CW01638728

OP 28

Military Interventions in Sierra Leone: Lessons From a Failed State

Larry J. Woods and Colonel Timothy R. Reese

Combat Studies Institute Press
US Army Combined Arms Center
Fort Leavenworth, Kansas

Library of Congress Cataloging-in-Publication Data

Woods, Larry J., 1949-
Military interventions in Sierra Leone : lessons from a failed state / Larry J. Woods and Timothy R. Reese.
p. cm. -- (The long war series)
Includes bibliographical references.
ISBN-13: 978-0-9801236-4-7
ISBN-10: 0-9801236-4-X
1. Sierra Leone--History--Civil War, 1991-2002. 2. Sierra Leone--History, Military. 3. Intervention (International law) 4. Failed states--Sierra Leone. I. Reese, Timothy R., 1959- II. Title. III. Series.

DT516.826.W66 2008
966.404--dc22

2008018715

First Printing: May 2008

Foreword

Recognizing the importance of the nations residing on the continent of Africa in an interconnected world, the United States established the United States Africa Command (USAFRICOM) in October 2007. That development alone makes it imperative that American military leaders understand the problems facing many African states today and the conflicts that have ravaged them in the recent past. Often rich in resources, both human and economic, yet uneven in development of governmental institutions and infrastructure, the nations of this large continent represent both a challenge and an opportunity. The challenge can be as complex as the removal of a sanctuary for terrorists without excessive violence or the marshalling of resources to alleviate a massive humanitarian crisis. The opportunity is that constructive engagement at an early stage can perhaps forestall the expenditure of large sums of blood and treasure to ameliorate a seriously deteriorating situation. In all of these cases, military leaders must have an understanding of Africa's geography, its peoples, and its history. Only through this understanding can the military instrument be applied intelligently and humanely.

This study by Larry J. Woods and Colonel Timothy R. Reese analyzes the massive turmoil afflicting the nation of Sierra Leone, 1995-2002, and the efforts by a variety of outside forces to bring lasting stability to that small country. The taxonomy of intervention ranged from private mercenary armies, through the Economic Community of West African States, to the United Nations and the United Kingdom. In every case, those who intervened encountered a common set of difficulties that had to be overcome. Unsurprisingly, they also discovered challenges unique to their own organizations and political circumstances. Serving soldiers can often profit vicariously from the mistakes of others as recounted in detailed case studies of historical events. This cogent analysis of recent interventions in Sierra Leone represents a cautionary tale that political leaders and military planners contemplating intervention in Africa ignore at their peril. *CSI—The Past is Prologue!*

William G. Robertson
Deputy Director, Combat Studies Institute

Acknowledgements

This Long War Occasional Paper could not have been written without the assistance of many individuals. Though the topic originated from the Combined Arms Center Research Priority List, it was the creation of the US Africa Command in October 2007 which provided the impetus to produce this study and to bring the military historical perspective to bear on this important region of the world. This is an unusual CSI publication in that we worked on this project as co-authors. We owe one another a debt for patience and cooperation along the path from concept development, research, writing and reviewing.

We would like to thank Mr. Michael Brooks for his patience, advice and hard work as our editor as he turned our text into a publishable study. Secondly, we would also like to thank Mr. Kendall D. Gott, Chief of the Research and Publications Team, for shepherding the overall process. Finally, we need to express our appreciation to Dr. William G. Robertson, Deputy Director of the Combat Studies Institute, for his advice, mentorship, and review of the first draft of this manuscript, as well as for his excellent foreword. We are indebted to each of them for their assistance, but any errors of fact or analysis are, of course, our responsibility.

Contents

Introduction

The country of Sierra Leone is located in Western Africa, bordering the North Atlantic Ocean between Guinea on the north and Liberia to the south (Map 1). It was little known to non-African specialists before the 1990s when it burst onto the world stage as the scene of more than a decade of brutal civil wars, the use of child soldiers, and widespread atrocities. Sierra Leone was labeled one of the classic examples of the so called "failed state syndrome" that theorists have used to describe nations which simply fail to function at the most elementary level. The anarchy in Sierra Leone led to outside military interventions and United Nations (UN) action in mostly vain attempts to end the human suffering. The attempts by the international community to do something about the human suffering in Sierra Leone during this period provide a multitude of lessons, both positive and negative, about attempts to deal with failed states.

The region of West Africa that later became Sierra Leone was dominated by two tribal societies, the Temne tribe in the north and the Mende

Map 1. Africa and Sierra Leone.

in the south, amidst a complex mix of ethnic groups making their living off of the land. In the era of European colonial rivalries that began in the mid 15th century, Portuguese, French, Dutch, Danish and British explorers, traders and colonialists competed for influence. In the early 17th century Europeans tapped into the existing slave trade and greatly expanded it to meet their demand for slaves in the New World. Great Britain outlawed slavery in its empire in 1807 and established a colony in the port of Freetown to enforce the decree in that part of West Africa. Over time Britain established Sierra Leone's borders and eventually created the Protectorate of Sierra Leone in 1896. Between 1896 and 1961 Great Britain controlled the Freetown Colony and oversaw the Protectorate. Despite borders which did not respect ancient tribal territories, and despite periods of internal ethnic strife, the Protcctorate prospered under relatively efficient British colonial rule. Great Britain granted the Freetown Colony and Sierra Leone their independence in April 1961. After independence and until 1992, a succession of ineffectual leaders alternated with a series of several "big men" who took their turns at attempting to knit a nation-state out of its fractured colonial heritage. Sierra Leone gradually fell victim to continued coups, corrupt and inefficient governments, and economic collapse.

Two of the so-called Big Men, Siaka Stevens and his successor General Joseph Momoh, ruled Sierra Leone for the 24 years between 1968 and 1992. Both men came from the ranks of the All Peoples Congress (APC), a political party led by ethnic Temnes. The APC was formed in opposition to the Sierra Leone Peoples Party (SLPP) which ruled Sierra Leone for the first seven years after independence and was dominated by members of the Mende tribe. The rule of the two Big Men was marked by mismanagement and corruption which left Sierra Leone in economic ruin, fostered ethnic conflict between the eighteen tribes that made up Sierra Leone, and placed the country in deep financial dependence upon foreign aid and loans. Both regimes used the country's chief natural resource, diamonds, as a source of money and power to enrich their own personal coffers. People who lived near the capital of Freetown and supported the reign of Stevens and Momoh lived somewhat more comfortably than the rest of the country which was isolated and agricultural.

Civil war broke out in 1991 when a rebel group, known as the Revolutionary United Front (RUF) launched a military offensive from neighboring Liberia to overthrow the Momoh government. An exiled Sierra Leonean named Foday Sankoh led the RUF forces. Sankoh organized the RUF movement in neighboring Liberia under the guidance of another infamous West African rebel, Charles Taylor. The RUF's political platform called for the overthrow of the Momoh government, the establishment of a multiparty democracy, and an end to economic exploitation. The RUF's idealistic platform soon gave way to the same corruption, misrule, and abuse of civilians as the Sierra Leonean government. RUF forces took over the diamond producing regions of Sierra Leone to finance their rebellion. The RUF was supported by the Taylor government in Liberia which wanted to cut off support to rebels opposed to his dictatorship operating from Sierra Leone. The diamond trade financed both the RUF and Taylor's forces and brought international interest to the civil war.

The RUF was particularly cruel, committing atrocities to include murder, rape, mutilation, abductions, and destruction of property on a vast scale. One of the RUF's most despicable techniques was the abduction of young children who were indoctrinated into the bizarre RUF ideology, then used as child soldiers to commit further atrocities. Life in Sierra Leone, already primitive, descended into an unimaginable chaos and suffering for nearly a dozen years after the 1991 civil war began. Roughly two million civilians fled to the neighboring countries of Guinea and Liberia, accounting for nearly a third of the population, and over 50,000 were killed. Cries for international actions to stop the civil war and alleviate the human suffering led to a succession of military interventions in Sierra Leone between 1992 and 2002 in attempts to restore order.

This Occasional Paper is a survey and analysis of the series of external military interventions in Sierra Leone between 1993 and 2002. Though each of these interventions achieved some local or temporary success, until late 2000 none of them succeeded in creating a security situation that could foster a political solution to Sierra Leone's woes. Each intervention ran afoul of Sierra Leone's ethnic divisions, ineffective and corrupt governments and meddling neighbor states. Equally important to the purposes of this study, each of these military interventions was hampered by internal problems and ineffectiveness. Since 2002 a fragile veneer of democratic normalcy has been in place, UN programs have disarmed more than 70,000 fighters, and the economy of Sierra Leone is recovering. Sierra Leone remains, however, one of the very poorest countries in the world by nearly every measure.

Chapter 1 provides a brief historical overview of Sierra Leone from its pre-colonial origins through 1992 and the start of a decade of civil war. Chapter 2 examines the years 1993 to 1997 during which the private military organization Executive Outcomes was called in by the Sierra Leone government in an attempt to restore order and stability. Chapter 3 looks at

Sierra Leone after 1997 when it again descended into chaos and analyzes the military intervention of the Economic Community of West African States (ECOWAS) and its military arm, led by its largest member, Nigeria. Chapter 4 reviews the international intervention led the by the UN and Great Britain between 1999 and 2002. Finally, Chapter 5 provides some conclusions and insights.

Chapter 1

The Road to External Interventions: Pre-Colonial Sierra Leone to 1992

Like many West African states, Sierra Leone has an intriguing history marked by unfulfilled potential and strife. This chapter will focus on the road to civil war in the 1990s and the era of external military interventions, briefly examining the political, social, and military situation. Tracing the history of this small country gives an idea of the complexity of the problems in Sierra Leone which are not unlike other states in this region of Africa.

Modern Sierra Leone is slightly smaller than the state of South Carolina with 70 miles of coastline and 27,925 square miles of land. The land is a mixture of mountains rising to 6,000 feet, wooded hills, swamps, and plateaus. A hilly peninsula dominates the western coast of Sierra Leone and together with the Sierra Leone river estuary, this region became the economic and political center of the region. It is a tropical environment with hot, rainy, humid summers from May to October and dry winters with a cold Saharan wind in December and January. Rainfall is plentiful on the coast and southern regions, but declines markedly in the northern grasslands.

Sierra Leone has 373 miles of navigable waterways with ports in Bonthe, Freetown, and Pepel. Its infrastructure is extremely limited with only 372 miles of paved highways; 7026 miles of unpaved highways; 52 miles of railways; and 10 airports covering the coast and inland areas, only one of which is paved at Lungi (near Freetown) with about 10,500 feet of paved runway.[1] The tropical landscape is an incubator for malaria, polio, yellow fever, river blindness, and other deadly diseases. With an estimated population of 6.14 million people, Sierra Leone is number 176 out of 177 on the United Nations Human Development Index, with life expectancies among the lowest in the world: Men born in Sierra Leone can expect to live to an average age of only 41, women to age 45.[2] Sierra Leone is rich in natural resources, including diamonds, gold, oil, iron ore, rutile, bauxite, and titanium. The economy consists of agriculture, exportation of raw materials and light local industry. As late as 2006, after three years of recovery from the dozen years of civil war examined in this study, the GDP of Sierra Leone was only $5.452 billion, yielding a per capital income of only $900. Only 35% of the population is literate.[3]

Origins

Before its discovery by Europeans, Sierra Leone was an agrarian society growing rice, millet, yams, coffee, cinnamon, and tobacco. It was characterized by nomadic ethnic tribes moving in and out of the area. Migration patterns reflected a search for fertile ground, warring factions among the ethnic tribes,[4] and the necessity for river transport.[5] By the late 1400s, some 18 ethnic groups had settled in the region, though they shared a common language with tribal dialects. The Mende tribe in the southern and eastern regions and the Temne tribe in the northern region dominated the mix.[6]

During this time tribal rulers were selected from those who were successful in battle and who could maintain stability in the villages. As the villages continued to grow, kings were selected from among the villagers. On the selection of a king elaborate ceremonies were conducted to link the king to the world of his ancestry and to receive the blessings of the transcendent authority. The king became the chief justice, land owner, and warlord and was expected to be proficient in divination, warfare, and hunting. In return his subjects were expected to pay tribute to him in the form of farm products and simple goods. The king relied heavily on his chiefs, elders, and other members of the ruling class.[7] The chiefs and elders had similar functions as the king, but in smaller tribal areas.

In 1462, Portuguese explorer Pedro da Cintra landed on the coast of Sierra Leone and mapped the hills surrounding the harbor, naming the formation Serra Lyoa or Lion Mountain. As more European explorers came to the area a small trading and mercantile class emerged to take its place alongside the agrarian society. A trade corridor grew among villages in the interior and the coastal area of West Africa. In the 1560s, British, French, Dutch, and Danish traders also landed in Africa. They became interested in the gold, cattle, salt, cloth, palm oil and rice of Sierra Leone. In the early 17th century the Europeans exploited the local practice of slavery to meet the massive demand for slaves to harvest cotton, rice, and sugar cane in the New World. In exchange for consumable goods, the kings, chiefs, and village rulers captured, sold, and traded slaves of all ages and genders.[8] Many of the slaves came from rival tribes as raids were conducted on neighboring villages. By 1652 slaves were being brought from Sierra Leone to the Caribbean and then onto plantations in South Carolina and Georgia where their rice-farming skills made them particularly valuable.[9] The British colonies in the New World were not the only area which employed slaves from Sierra Leone. About 80 percent of the local peoples enslaved from Sierra Leone were shipped to the Caribbean and Brazil. This heinous trade lasted for over 100 years.

Competing religious beliefs further complicated Sierra Leonean society during pre-colonial times. Christianity was introduced by Catholic missionaries from Portugal. Islam came to Sierra Leone primarily through commercial traders from Arabia and Persia. Both Christianity and Islam flourished, but both were heavily influenced by local pre-monotheistic practices. Many villages kept their practice of worshipping nature that included mountains and trees and some held to animistic beliefs. A very common item of worship were icons, such as soapstone figurines, that were worn to either ward off bad spirits or provide good luck for some temporal situation such as fertility or battle.[10]

European Colonialism

In 1807 Great Britain outlawed slavery throughout its vast empire with the passage of the Slave Trade Act. As a result of the desire to repatriate slaves to their former land, the British sent 331 freed slaves, 61 white female London prostitutes, and several English tradesmen from Nova Scotia and Britain to Sierra Leone. Upon arrival, Captain Thomas Thompson purchased a piece of uninhabited land from the local Temne chief on the northern end of what would become known as the Freetown Peninsula.[11] Although half of the ex-slaves died within a year because of disease and tribal wars, this British enclave survived. To improve the settlement's chances of longevity for freed slaves, the British government purchased another piece of land near the coast and established a settlement known as Freetown. In 1808, Freetown became one of Britain's first colonies in West Africa.[12]

The British Government took responsibility for Freetown and used its naval assets to intercept slave ships of other nations along the West African coast. Freetown quickly grew in population with both freed slaves and "recaptives," those liberated from the ships. Since the population was a mixture of cultures and languages, and the former slaves were cut off from their homes and traditions, they assimilated many aspects of the British style of life. Part of this assimilation was the result of Anglican and Methodist missionaries from Britain and the United States who brought the English language and Christianity to Sierra Leone.[13] An ethnic group unto themselves, they were known as Creoles. Education was readily available from Christian missionaries, so the Creoles became a vibrant group of educated professionals including doctors, lawyers, traders, and businessmen. They also rose to hold low and mid-level positions in the British colonial government.

As a British colony Freetown was expected to pay for itself and contribute to the economic health of the Empire, primarily through exports.[14] The hinterland regions outside the city of Freetown became the focus of the British Government upon the realization that its rich resources could turn a profit. Although disputes over territorial boundaries existed for decades, the British Government reached an agreement in 1896 with the neighboring countries of French Guinea and Liberia to establish its territorial borders. Soon after the agreement was signed the British Government declared the region a protectorate of the British government. Effectively, the British now ruled two entities in the same region: the Freetown Colony and the Protectorate which included the hinterland (Map 2).

Map 2. Sierra Leone.

The establishment of the British Protectorate enraged the native chiefs, primarily because the Protectorate was divided into districts which did not correspond to ancient tribal lands. The chiefs had not been consulted about this arrangement and were informed that they now worked for a district commissioner who was appointed by the colony. The Temne and Mende chiefs and their respective tribes immediately rebelled against colonial rule, slaughtering settlers and missionaries, policemen and Creoles, without differentiating between them. In response to this rebellion, the Freetown Colony established a Frontier Police Force, composed of Creoles, Protectorate citizens, and former British Army soldiers. The Frontier Police Force was met with much opposition outside the Freetown Colony for the tribal chiefs—who were formerly recognized as African kings—were now designated merely as "paramount chiefs."[15] The Freetown Colony ruled the hinterland through these paramount chiefs and expected them to comply with the instructions provided by the Frontier Police Force.

The Freetown Colony established a tribal tax, known as the hut tax, to fund the Frontier Police Force and other activities of the administration, to include paying the paramount chiefs. The military governor, Colonel Frederic Cardew, decreed that the inhabitants of the Protectorate should be taxed on the size of their huts.[16] The hut tax sparked two rebellions in 1898, one by the Temne, led by Bai Bureh, and the other by the Mende, led by Momoh Jah. In January 1898, Bai Bureh, a tribal king, and his chiefs refused to pay hut taxes. Consequently, Colonel Cardew sent the Frontier Police Force, backed by a battalion of government soldiers, to collect the taxes in each of the villages. If a local chief refused to make payment, the police force often destroyed the rice fields, crops, and huts, while terrorizing the inhabitants. Bai Bureh's village militias employed stockades built of palm logs, embedded in the ground and buttressed with red dirt to defend their territories. Bai Bureh and his soldiers lay behind the stockade protected in trenches, and fired through openings in the logs. British troops were eventually able to overcome the stockades and capture Bai Bureh. By the end of May 1898, the Frontier Police had destroyed 97 towns and villages and deprived Bai Bureh of his food supply.[17] Bureh, upon his capture, was immediately deported to Ghana.

A second anti-British rebellion broke out among the Mende in April 1898, after the arrest of Momoh Jah, the Mende paramount chief. Runners were dispatched to various villages and told to defend their land and refuse to pay the hut tax. Christian missionaries in the Mende country, trying to avoid bloodshed, advocated paying the hut tax and solving the issue through peaceful means. The villagers took this as an official alignment with the government, and the missionaries soon found themselves under attack.[18] The Freetown administration launched two military expeditions to crush the rebellion and by the end of the war hundreds of government and tribal members were killed. The Freetown Colony brought 158 tribal leaders and others to trial and executed 96 of the leaders.[19] Following the trials and the executions Freetown Soldiers marched through the villages carrying the British flag as a reminder to the villagers of British authority. This pattern of violence between the more prosperous and settled area around Freetown and the rural countryside continues to this day.

Smaller scale resistance and local uprisings continued against the British colony in Freetown but each one failed because of British military superiority. Most of the early 1900s was unremarkable and the colony was relatively peaceful. The economy thrived during the mid 20th century with large exports of diamonds, palm kernels, coffee, cocoa, and iron. These commodities provided the Colony and the Protectorate with a relatively buoyant economy.

British explorers discovered diamonds in Sierra Leone in 1930 during a routine geological survey of the Kono District in eastern Sierra Leone. More surveys in 1933 and 1934 found diamonds along the length of the Sewa River, as well as at various portions of the Moa River basin to the south. Shortly after these discoveries, the Colonial Government created the Sierra Leone Selection Trust (SLST), granting this division of the DeBeers Corporation exclusive prospecting and mining license covering the whole of Sierra Leone.[20]

In the early 1950s the practice of illegal diamond mining was already prevalent in the Kono area. Between 1952 and 1955, hundreds of thousands of people rushed to the region threatening to destabilize the economy and the country. In 1955 the government imposed a two-fold solution to correct the problems, bring order to the region, and restore its tax system on which it was heavily dependent. The SLST was ordered to confine its mining activities to specific areas while the remainder of the known diamond fields were licensed to independent diggers. In 1956 the government also decided to expel all non-Sierra Leoneans from the Kono district. This action, coordinated with neighboring French colonial authorities and supported by the local chiefs and the Sierra Leonean political class, expelled an estimated 45,000 people from the region.[21]

During and after World War II, Sierra Leone consistently exported over million carats of official diamonds per year contributing the vast majority of revenue for the colony. In 1957, SLST surveyors found new diamond resources in the Bo District of Sierra Leone and began to bring them into production. Mining, both official and illegal, was conducted with almost no regard to its environmental impact. Finally, the large sums of money that could be made in the diamond industry, when contrasted with the underpaid and inefficient bureaucracy of Sierra Leone, provided fertile breeding grounds for corruption.[22]

Sierra Leone's prosperity was used by the British to establish regional schools, build roads into the countryside, and to begin delivering rudimentary health care.[23] Consistent with the British decision to dissolve much of the Empire after World War II, power was gradually moved from British officials to elected Sierra Leoneans between 1951 and 1961. The British oversaw the creation of political parties, local, regional and then national governmental institutions.

Independence

On 27 April 1961, the United Kingdom granted Sierra Leone its independence with a parliamentary system within the British Commonwealth. Sir Milton Margai, an ethnic Mende physician, was appointed the first Prime Minister. Margai led the Sierra Leone People's Party (SLPP) to victory in the first general election in May 1962. After Sir Milton's death in 1964, his half-brother, Sir Albert Margai, succeeded him as Prime Minister. The initial ethnic balance in government established by the British upon independence soon gave way. Margai quickly moved to install members of the Mende tribe in all key positions. For example, Margai increased the representation of the Mende in the Army's officer ranks from 26 percent to 52 percent of the total.[24] This upset the delicate ethnic balance for the Mende and Temne each represented about 30 percent of the total population of Sierra Leone. It soon became apparent, through the passage of various laws and personnel appointments, that the Margai government strongly favored the Mende at the expense of other groups. Ethnic and regional tensions seethed beneath the calm exterior.

With growing popular resentment against the Mende-dominated SLPP, the All People's Congress (APC) party led by Siaka Stevens, won the majority of seats in the national elections on 17 March 1967. Siaka Stevens, an ethnic Temne, was thus scheduled to become the new Prime Minister of Sierra Leone. But as Stevens was about to take office on 21 March, a military coup d'etat was launched by Brigadier David Lansana, a Temne Army officer who had Stevens arrested. Lansana also took control of the radio stations and declared martial law, but his rule was short lived. On 23 March a group of army officers launched a successful counter coup under the banner of the National Reformation Council (NRC) and deposed Lansana.[25] Finally, a group of noncommissioned soldiers calling themselves the National Interim Council (NIC) ousted the NRC in a second counter-coup in April 1968. On 26 April 1968, the NIC returned control of the government to Siaka Stevens who was sworn in as Prime Minister—a year and two coups after he was elected.

Stevens moved quickly to establish his power and the power of the Temne tribes under the political cover of the APC party. He replaced cabinet members and senior members of the army with men of Temne ethnicity. Stevens had the senior Mende officers and the police leadership arrested and replaced them with his trusted soldiers. By May 1968, almost all Mende officers were purged from the army and replaced by Temne officers. To obtain a position in the army, all recruits had to swear allegiance to the new Temne dominated government.[26]

Siaka Stevens remained in control for 18 years. He saw himself as a "Big Man," an African term for the most important person in the state. Over the years Siaka destroyed the remaining vestiges of democracy and ethnic cooperation in Sierra Leone. In 1971 he changed the political system from a parliamentary system to a republic and declared himself executive president. In 1978, Stevens established a one-party state ruled by the APC, effectively making him a dictator. Political opposition leaders and conspirators were arrested, tried, and executed. Newspaper presses were destroyed and the editors and publishers were killed if they printed unwelcome news.[27] Such was the repressive nature of the state during Stevens' reign.

The Ceremonial Army

Having had his Presidency delayed for a year by a military coup, Stevens distrusted the army even though he had imprisoned most of his opposition shortly after taking office. Because of his paranoia of another military coup, Stevens developed his own security division, known as the Internal Security Unit (ISU), as part of the police force guarding the capital. Stevens used it primarily as an instrument of tyranny and suppression for his one-party state. The ISU became a paramilitary wing of the Sierra Leone Police (SLP) and received training in Guinea and in Cuba. Stevens ensured that it enjoyed far better pay, equipment and training than the regular army.

Under both Stevens and his successor Joseph Momoh, the Republic of Sierra Leone Military Forces (RSLMF) were riddled with factional rivalries and were largely incompetent as a military force. It was essentially a ceremonial army.[28] The army, for the most part, did not even have weapons.[29] Nepotism and party affiliation were the basis for selecting leaders; merit and dedication to one's duties were of little importance in rising through the ranks. Officers who engaged in political sycophancy or tribal connections were the ones most likely to advance in their careers. The army did not conduct regular training exercises and officers rarely ventured into the field.[30] Junior soldiers routinely went without pay for several months whereas the senior officers often sold the rations of their soldiers for profit.

The army consisted of some 3,000 soldiers organized into two battalions. The First Battalion was made up of some 1,000 old soldiers whose service dated from the immediate post colonial days. The Second Battalion of about 500 to 600 personnel was located near the capital and two training units operated at Daru and Benguema.[31] The army also lacked modern equipment such as armored vehicles, supply trucks, communication equipment and helicopters.

Economic Collapse and the End of the Stevens Era

Sierra Leone's primary source of foreign exchange is natural resources, one of which was rutile, a titanium mineral used in guided missiles, jewelry, and a variety of manufactured goods. Sierra Leone also contained usable gold deposits and diamonds. The Sierra Leone Selection Trust (SLST) Company, part of the De Beers cartel, dominated the diamond mining industry and provided the money used by Stevens to finance his regime. In 1971, Stevens created the Diamond Mining Company (DIMINCO), which effectively nationalized SLST. All important decisions were now made by the Prime Minister and his right hand man, a Lebanese businessman named Jamil Mohammed.[32] Private companies sponsored by corrupt government officials diverted the mineral trade for their own benefits and bankrupted the state treasury leaving the country in dire straits. From a high of over two million carats officially exported in 1970, legitimate diamond exports dropped to 595,000 carats in 1980 and then to only 48,000 in 1988.[33] Since diamonds were easy to smuggle, one study estimated that 97 percent of diamonds from Sierra Leone were carried out of the country illegally in the 1980s.[34]

The elderly Stevens stepped down in 1985 and nominated General

Joseph Momoh, the head of the RSLMF, as his successor. Momoh was the only candidate in a one-party election and as a member of the APC Party he was elected by a very large margin. Upon taking office, Momoh declared a state of economic emergency, which granted him even greater control over Sierra Leone's economy than was enjoyed by his predecessor. Momoh proved corrupt, weak, and inept as a leader. Sierra Leone's economy quickly disintegrated and the country's currency became essentially worthless. The failing economy led to the collapse of government services as civil servants went unpaid, schools simply ceased to operate and the basic infrastructure of the state collapsed. Because the government could not afford to import gasoline and fuel oil, the country often went without electricity for months.[35] In the midst of the slow dissolution of political and economic life in Sierra Leone, a new force entered the picture that would dominate Sierra Leone's affairs for the next decade.

The Revolutionary United Front

Sierra Leone's strife gave birth to numerous opposition and rebel movements in the 1980s and 1990s. Former army corporal Foday Sankoh stands out as the most important among that undistinguished group. An ethnic Temne, he served in the RSLMF in the early 1970s and had obtained the rank of corporal. Upon leaving the army, he worked as a TV cameraman, but was fired for insubordination. He then became a freelance photographer while attending Freetown College. In college, he became a student activist and demonstrated against the government.[36] Sankoh was briefly imprisoned in the 1970s and upon his release he declared that he would seek revenge on the ruling APC government.

He joined other West African dissidents in Libya where Colonel Muammar al-Gaddafi was sponsoring revolutionary movements throughout the world. Sankoh later went to Liberia, where he joined forces with another young and charismatic revolutionary leader, Charles Taylor, whom he had met in Libya. It was in Liberia that Sankoh further developed his revolutionary ideas and bizarre tactics. Taylor launched a brutal civil war in neighboring Liberia in 1989. Sankoh participated in the earliest stages of the Liberian civil wars and Taylor noticed his leadership abilities.

Taylor was also seeking revenge against the Momoh government of Sierra Leone. Momoh was allowing the Lungi airport near Freetown to be used by soldiers from the Economic Community of West African States Military Observer Group (ECOMOG) in support of Taylor's rivals in Liberia, the United Liberian Movement for Democracy (ULIMO). Momoh had also deployed the one operational battalion of the Sierra Leonean Army, known as the Leone Battalion (LEOBATT), to participate in ECOMOG forces that intervened in Liberia in 1990 in a futile attempt to end that civil war.[37] Taylor thought a revolutionary force in the eastern and southeastern part of Sierra Leone would provide a buffer zone to impede the progress of ECOMOG and ULIMO while he took control of Liberia.[38] Taylor also took notice of the rich diamond mines in Sierra Leone.

Sankoh began assembling his revolutionary force in October 1990 as he was traveling to varying locations on the western border of Liberia. Detention centers and refugee camps populated by a mix of Sierra Leoneans and other nationalities served as the source of manpower for Taylor, and Sankoh adopted the technique. Taylor's National Patriotic Front of Liberia (NPFL) fighters would beat, molest, and execute civilians in the camps to obtain recruits and information. As Sankoh visited these areas, he would separate the Sierra Leoneans from the rest of the group and blackmail them into becoming members of the Revolutionary United Front (RUF) in return for shielding them from the NPFL.[39] Sankoh was also a charismatic leader, however, and he persuaded many displaced Sierra Leoneans to join his cause voluntarily. Many Sierra Leoneans were drawn to this revolutionary movement which appeared to offer an attractive solution to the ethnic conflicts and economic ruin that was Sierra Leone in 1991.

Sankoh launched his first incursions into Sierra Leone from Liberia in late March and early April 1991 into the districts of Kailahun on the eastern border and Pujehun on the southern border. These incursions concentrated on capturing land, civilians, towns, and equipment. The force was led by the special forces of Taylor's NPFL and the vanguard of the RUF.[40] Of the 2000 attackers, about 1600 came from Liberian forces and 400 came from Sierra Leone. Sakoh organized his forces into two battalions, each with three companies of approximately 60 members each.[41]

NPFL and RUF forces launched their eastern attack from the Liberian town of Foya Kamal, attacking down the main highway from the western edge towards the interior of Sierra Leone. Their initial objective was to clear the road to Koindu and then to wait for reinforcements to continue to advance.[42] Their ultimate objective was to capture the strategic military barracks, known as Moa Barracks, in the town of Daru located on the Moa River.[43] If the insurgents could capture Moa Barracks they could use it as a base for their own operations as they moved south toward Kenema while denying it as a base for the Sierra Leone Army.

The insurgents crossed the border in trucks, modified vans, 4x4 vehicles and by foot. They were armed with a mix of small arms, machine guns, and rocket propelled grenades (RPG) but lacked heavy weapons or air support.[44] The RUF dressed in a bizarre combination of camouflage and civilian clothes laced with charms such as shells, nets, wigs, face paints, and religious symbols. The attackers encountered very little resistance because RSLMF troops in the area quickly retreated due to lack of motivation and ammunition. As the NPFL and RUF combatants moved toward Koindu they went on looting sprees and indiscriminately killed many civilians. As word spread to other villages about these attacks, large numbers of civilians sought refuge in neighboring Guinea and Liberia.

Unbeknownst to the attackers, however, ECOMOG forces supporting the Liberian government had arrived at Moa Barracks to establish a

Map 3. RUF offensives, 1991.

forward operating base in eastern Sierra Leone. The ECOMOG contingent consisted of only 200 troops from the Guinean Armed Forces (GAF), but they brought considerable firepower to include artillery and air support. As the lightly equipped NPFL and RUF forces numbering about 1,000 approached Koindu from the east they were routed by the more heavily armed and disciplined Guinean troops.[45] The offensive ground to a halt.

As the eastern attack stalled, the combined NPLF and RUF incursion on the southern front in the Pujehun District met with greater success. They were able to quickly capture the bridge over the Mano River that provided the rebels with unlimited access into the region. They plundered and captured many towns and villages as they pushed toward the Bo District, containing the second largest city in Sierra Leone. The insurgents met with very little resistance from scattered RMSLF outposts and were initially welcomed by the inhabitants of many villages in the district.[46] Most Sierra Leoneans were initially happy to see an alternative to the mistreatment and corruption of the government. These two offensives were forerunners of a decade of scattered fighting between rag-tag military forces, wide spread use of armed civilians as soldiers, indiscriminate attacks on civilians, and massive refugee flows that came to dominate Sierra Leone for the next ten years.

Local Response to Invasion: The Civil Defense Forces and the *Kamajors*

In response to the attacks by the rebel and the lack of support from the army, many loyal towns and villages formed paramilitary units and militias that would eventually become known as Civil Defense Forces (CDF). One type of CDF were known as *kamajor* units. The *kamajors* were selected by the paramount chiefs and were known for their ability to hunt and trap wild animals. Originally paramount chiefs selected only two *kamajors* per village, but as the civil war progressed, the need for more *kamajors* became important. The *kamajors* mixed self defense with mysticism and inculcated a cult of invincibility. They required their candidates to be initiated in secret ceremonies to further their sacrosanct beliefs. In the beginning, the only weapons they had were machetes, swords, paddles, and rocks to fend off the rebels. Using captured NPLF and RUF weapons and equipment they soon became a formidable force, actually outnumbering the rebel army in some parts of the country.

Due to their success in combating the RUF forces, the government incorporated the *kamajor* CDF units into to the state security system. While this had the effect of combating the RUF invasion, it further denigrated the army's status and diverted resources badly needed to rejuvenate its ability to conduct operations.[47] CDF units were locally based and thus could not effectively operate outside their local areas. As the *kamajors* grew in numbers, they succumbed to the general lawlessness and lack of discipline that plagued every aspect of Sierra Leonean society and government. The paramount chief initially chose the *kamajors* in each village based on their abilities and therefore held some control over their actions. As they grew in number, however, the *kamajor* began recruiting their own members. Soon, significant numbers of urban street gang members were drawn into the CDF, as were many deserters from the RUF and RSLMF. Soon the *kamajor* CDF units were involved in corruption, extortion, mistreatment or murder of captives, and brutality towards civilians unfortunate enough to be caught in the fighting.

The RUF in Sierra Leone

Tension between the RUF and the NFPL leadership eventually became so intense that Taylor decided to remove his troops from Sierra Leone. As the NFPL troops left they took all of their weapons and ammunition with them leaving Sankoh and the RUF in a vulnerable situation. Sankoh and his soldiers had captured some equipment from the RSLMF, but not enough to sustain operations. Sankoh and the RUF soon discovered the importance and value of diamonds. As Sankoh and his soldiers took over mining areas in southern Sierra Leone, he found himself with a product he could barter. Sankoh approached Taylor about an exchange and Taylor was interested. Taylor needed a way to finance his operations in Liberia and diamonds were a commodity not easily traced. He established a network of illegal buyers and sellers from various countries and was able to smuggle weapons and ammunition to barter with Sankoh and to support his war.

Diamonds became the principle means to fund the war in Sierra Leone for both sides. Diamonds were easy to transport, hide, and easy to convert into cash. They were virtually impossible to detect in airports and untraceable as to origin.[48] Controlling the mines allowed millions of dollars worth of diamonds to change hands in order to purchase and trade for equipment, weapons, and medical supplies. The presence of alluvial diamonds made it easy for the RUF to channel illegal diamonds to Liberia. Since alluvial diamonds were not mined in the traditional sense, but rather by "panning" in much the same way as miners "panned for gold," it made it easy to extract them and carry them to buyers in other countries.[49] The

RUF enslaved thousands of civilians and made them work the mines. If the workers didn't meet their quota or tried to steal diamonds, they were often executed and dumped in shallow graves.[50]

A diamond network was developed from Sierra Leone, going through Liberia and/or Guinea, and then on to Antwerp, Belgium; Bombay, India; or New York City using a variety of Lebanese merchants.[51] The Lebanese had settled in Sierra Leone in the wake of World War II and opened up many import-export shops selling consumer goods, general merchandise, and electronic products from around the world. Many of these Lebanese merchants exchanged goods for diamonds. If a diamond certificate of authenticity was necessary to identify the country's origin and legitimacy, bribes would be made to customs officials and certificates issued. The scale of the diamonds taken from Sierra Leone and sold through the illicit trade networks was staggering. Although Liberia could only produce 200,000 carats of industrial diamonds from its own resources, it exported over 6 million carats a year.[52]

The RUF had several objectives in addition to financing and equipping its forces, but three were most significant: crippling Sierra Leone's commercial and industrial activities, undermining the physical security of the state, and attracting international publicity.[53] Sankoh believed that if he could deny diamond revenues to the state, then he could cripple the government and force a negotiation between the RUF and the government. He carried out raids and ambushes on state controlled diamond mining operations after carefully assessing the situation. He used intelligence information gathered from local infiltrators—often children—and conducted stakeouts to ensure success.[54] If Sankoh could stop mining operations, he could cripple the state's revenue.

Second, the RUF whittled away at the Sierra Leone Army and undermined its credibility. As the RUF captured equipment, its members would dress up in their confiscated army uniforms, move into civilian villages and towns, and conduct operations. Civilians, thinking they were part of the army, let them into their villages and soon found themselves victims of property destruction, mass killings, brutality, rape, and kidnapping. The RUF intentionally spread confusion and terror among the civilian population while blaming the army for it.[55]

Finally, Sankoh wanted to attract international attention for the RUF's armed struggle and to be part of the negotiation process. Sankoh believed that if he could make life unbearable in Sierra Leone, it would lead the

government to the negotiating table.[56] He believed that if he could persuade the media favorably toward his revolution, then he could eventually have a part in the new government.

Child Soldiers

The RUF, the RSLMF, and the CDF all adopted the horrific practice of using young children as young as 7 as soldiers during the civil war. Since 55 percent of the population was under 18 the supply of child soldiers was plentiful. Many of the child soldiers were abandoned, captured in raids, or their parents were killed by the RUF. They were hungry, and needed care and a place to live. All three military forces eagerly "adopted" them. Many children were initially used as load-bearers who carried ammo, equipment, and food to supply the fighters who had taken them captive. Soon, however, children were taught to fire weapons by their captors and placed on the front lines. Some children fought for revenge. They had lost their family and friends at the hands of rebel forces and had watched their homes burn to the ground. Other children joined the army to feel safe; they needed to feel part of some family social structure and the army provided the basics of food, shelter, clothing, and camaraderie in arms. Ishmael Beah, a child soldier, provided the following account in his now famous memoirs:

> I am from Sierra Leone, and the problem that is affecting us children is the wars that force us to run away from our homes, lose our families, and aimlessly roam the forests. As a result, we get involved in the conflict as soldiers, carriers of loads, and in many other difficult tasks. All this is because of starvation, the loss of our families, and the need to feel safe and be part of something when all else has broken down. I joined the army really because of the loss of my family and starvation. I wanted to avenge the death of my family. I also had to get some food to survive, and the only way to do that was to be part of the army. It was not easy being a soldier, but we just had to do it.[57]

It was estimated that over half of the RUF combatants were between the ages of seven and fifteen, both male and female. RUF commanders often preferred to use child soldiers because children were fearless, compliant, and easier to manipulate. A child could be sent into a crowd without suspicion and have him collect intelligence, or have him throw a grenade at soldiers. Children were also considered expendable because they did not have families. There was a division of labor between the sexes; boys were used as fighters and miners whereas girls were used for cooking, transporting, and sex.

All sides in the war treated captives with extreme brutality. In his memoir, Beah described how a lieutenant from the RSLMF taught his child soldiers how to practice killing prisoners. He brought in five RUF prisoners with hands tied behind their backs and lined them up before the child soldiers. He instructed the child soldiers, upon command, to slice the throat of a prisoner while looking at the prisoner's face. The winner of the contest was the prisoner who died first.[58] Ruthless, senseless killing was the standard during the civil war and much occurred at the hands of child soldiers.

To prevent children from escaping their captors, many were often tattooed, scarred, or branded. If they tried to escape, they would often face death at the hands of soldiers or CDF or even village lynch mobs who would recognize the symbols displayed on the child soldier's body. If they were recaptured by their own group, they were often made an example. As described by one boy, age fifteen,

> One boy tried to escape, but he was caught. His hands were tied, and then they made us, the other new captives, kill him with a stick. I felt sick. I knew this boy from before. We were from the same village. I refused to kill him and they told me they would shoot me. They pointed a gun at me, so I had to do it. The boy was asking me, "Why are you doing this?" I said I had no choice. After we killed him, they made us smear his blood on our arms. I felt dizzy. I felt so sick. They said we had to do this so we would not fear death and so we would not try to escape.[59]

Though the RSLMF and the CDF treated children and captives with brutality, the RUF was by far the biggest violator of human rights in Sierra Leone.

Summary

By 1992, the insurrection had taken a terrible toll on Sierra Leone. The RUF offensive had been halted, but they remained in control of large swaths of territory. Since the eastern and southern regions of Sierra Leone were the breadbaskets of the country, food production was severely disrupted. Many towns and villages were burned to the ground by both sides during the fighting. Tens of thousands of refugees left Sierra Leone for neighboring Guinea to live in squalid refugee camps. The RUF rebels successfully occupied the diamond mining area of Kono in eastern Sierra Leone depriving the state of its prime source of revenue and financing their own illicit trade. Though he was able to gain initial popular support for his campaign against the government, Sankoh's revolutionary movement soon lost credibility and support because of RUF brutality and corruption.[60] Sankoh's diamond mining operations, his bizarre attempts to draw attention to his movement, and the brutality of his tactics reduced the population of Sierra Leone to a Hobbsian state of existence. The ineffectual leadership of General Momoh in the face of the RUF invasion weakened his hold on the army and the APC party. Valentine Strasser, a 29-year-old army captain, overthrew General Momoh in a military coup in April 1992.[61] International human rights organizations, neighboring countries and the United Nations soon demanded action to end the suffering, opening ten years of military interventions.

Notes

1. Central Intelligence Agency, "CIA World Factbook–Sierra Leone," https://www.cia.gov/library/publications/the-world-factbook/geos/sl.html (accessed 18 June 2007).

2. United Nations, *Human Development Reports*, http://hdr.undp.org/hdr2006/statistics/countries/country_fact_sheets/cty_fs_SLE.html (accessed 20 June 2007).

3. Central Intelligence Agency, "CIA World Factbook–Sierra Leone," https://www.cia.gov/library/publications/the-world-factbook/geos/sl.html (accessed 18 June 2007).

4. Properly used, the word "tribe" in Africa refers to an ethnic group, but ethnicity is not rigidly bounded; it changes over time and overlaps with other identities. No single criterion always works to determine ethnicity or to distinguish between ethnic groups, but the criteria in Africa are language difference and geographical place of ancestral origin.

5. Earl Conteh-Morgan and Mac Dixon-Fyle, *Sierra Leone at the End of the Twentieth Century*, (New York: Peter Lang Publishing, Inc, 1999), 11-15.

6. Alexander Peter Kup, *Sierra Leone*, (New York: St. Martin's Press, 1975), 41-113. These two chapters are excellent resources for the history of the Mende and Temne ethnic groups. The Temne have been around Sierra Leone the longest, but the Mende are the largest ethnic group in Sierra Leone today.

7. Conteh-Morgan and Dixon-Fyle, *Sierra Leone at the End of the Twentieth Century*, 18-19.

8. The Atlantic slave trade is marked by the high point of unequal exchange between European traders and Sierra Leone counterparts, often chiefs of villages. The loss of manpower left the area without the means to produce their own land. It is interesting that as the slave trade moves forward, the exchange of slaves for guns becomes the most important trade. Put in another way, trading capital goods (slaves produce other slaves) for consumable goods.

9. US Department of State, Bureau of American Affairs, *Background Note: Sierra Leone*, http://www.state.gov/r/pa/ei/bgn/5475.htm (accessed 13 June 2007).

10. Conteh-Morgan and Dixon-Fyle, *Sierra Leone at the End of the Twentieth Century*, 13.

11. Simon Schama, *Rough Crossings: Britain, the Slaves and the American Revolution*, (United Kingdom: Ecco Press, 2006).

12. John L. Hirsch, *Sierra Leone: Diamonds and the Struggle for Democracy*, (Boulder, CO: Lynne Rienner Publishers, 2001), 22-25.

13. Alexander Peter Kup, *Sierra Leone*, 114-117, and 156-160.

14. Kenneth P. Vickery, *The African Experience From "Lucy" to Mandela* Course No. 8678. The Teaching Company. CD-ROM. 2007.

15. Conteh-Morgan and Dixon-Fyle, *Sierra Leone at the End of the Twentieth Century*, 41. The paramount chiefs, in the long run retained much of their local authority, but they staunchly opposed it.

16. Arthur Abraham, "Mende Government and Politics Under Colonial Rule: A Historical Study of Political Change in Sierra Leone 1890-1937," *The International Journal of African Historical Studies*, VII, 1, (1974), http://www.jstor.org/sici?sici=0361-7882(1982)15%3A2%3C297%3AMGAPUC%3E2.0.CO%3B2-H (accessed 18 June 2007).

17. Ibid.

18. Richard Gott, "Sierra Leone and New Labor Militarism," *Z Magazine*, http://www.zmag.org/crisiscurevts/sierra_leone.htm (accessed 18 June 2007).

19. Ibid.

20. Jim William, Donald Sutherland, Kimberly Cartwright and Martin Byrnes, *Sierra Leone Diamond Policy Study*, AMCO-Robertson Mineral Services, Ltd. (January 2002), http://www.reliefweb.int/library/documents/2002/dfid_sle_diamond.pdf (accessed 23 April 2008).

21. Ibid.

22. Ibid.

23. David Pratt, MP, *Sierra Leone: The Forgotten Crisis*, report to Canadian Minister of Foreign Affairs, Lloyd Axworthy, PC, MP, 23 April 1999.

24. Conteh-Morgan and Dixon-Fyle, *Sierra Leone at the End of the Twentieth Century*, 78.

25. Abass Bundu, *Democracy by Force?: A Study of International Military Intervention in the Conflict in Sierra Leone from 1991-2000*, (London: Universal Publishers, 2001), 41-43.

26. David Keen, *Conflict and Collusion in Sierra Leone*, (New York: Palgrave Publishers, 2005), 14-15. At the time, free bags of rice were given to army soldiers and this made any "buy-in" a lucrative deal. The rice was either used for family needs or sold to others. The selling of rice became very profitable for senior army leaders.

27. Conteh-Morgan and Dixon-Fyle, *Sierra Leone at the End of the Twentieth Century*, 80-81.

28. Thomas S. Cox, *Civil Military Relations in Sierra Leone: A Case Study of African Soldiers in Politics*, (Cambridge, MA: Harvard University Press, 1976), 207.

29. Keen, *Conflict and Collusion in Sierra Leone*, 17. Most of the rifles were antiquated.

30. Truth and Reconciliation Commission of Sierra Leone, *Final Report of the Truth and Reconciliation Commission of Sierra Leone*, Chapter 3, para 245, http://trcsierraleone.org/drwebsite/publish/v3a-c1.shtml (accessed 26 July 2007).

31. Ibid., para 246.

32. Victor A. B. Davies, *Will Sierra Leone Grow Again?*; available from http://

www.gdnet.org/pdf/draft_country_studies/SierraLeone-DaviesFR.pdf (accessed 10 June 2007).

33. M. A. Sesay, "Interdependence and Dependency in the Political Economy of Sierra Leone." PhD. diss, University of Southampton, 1993, 295-319, 21.

34. Ian Smillie, Lansana Gberie and Ralph Hazleton, "The Heart of the Matter: Sierra Leone, Diamonds & Human Security" *Insights, Partnership Africa Canada*, January 2000, http://www.sierra-leone.org/heartmatter.html (accessed 8 June 2007).

35. Hirsch, *Sierra Leone: Diamonds and the Struggle for Democracy*, 30-31.

36. Kwaku Nuarmah and William Zartman, "Intervention in Sierra Leone," in *Military Intervention: Cases in Context for the Twenty-First Century*, William J. Lahneman (New York: Rowmann and Littlefield, 2004), 133-150.

37. Ibid., para 248.

38. Keen, *Conflict and Collusion in Sierra Leone*, 36-38.

39. Truth and Reconciliation Commission of Sierra Leone, *Final Report of the Truth and Reconciliation Commission of Sierra Leone*, Chapter 3, http://trcsierraleone.org/drwebsite/publish/v3a-c1.shtml (accessed 8 June 2007).

40. The term "Special Forces" is understood to denote fighters who have been trained outside of the country they are fighting in. It is not due to specialized training. The vanguards were selected and trained by Sankoh.

41. Hirsch, *Sierra Leone: Diamonds and the Struggle for Democracy*, 145.

42. Truth and Reconciliation Commission of Sierra Leone, *Final Report of the Truth and Reconciliation Commission of Sierra Leone*, para 159.

43. Ibid., para. 221-222.

44. Ibid., para. 161.

45. Ibid.

46. Ibid.

47. Truth and Reconciliation Commission of Sierra Leone, *Final Report of the Truth and Reconciliation Commission of Sierra Leone*.

48. Eunice Ajambo, "Debate Over al Qaeda's Connection to West Africa's Diamond Trade Takes New Turns," *allAfrica.com*, 5 August 2004, http://allafrica.com/stories/printable/200408050800.html (accessed 12 June 2007).

49. Sierra Leone Web, "Testimony of Joseph Melrose, 13 February 02," http://www.sierra-leone.org/melrose021301.html (accessed 15 June 2007).

50. Greg Campbell, *Blood Diamonds: Tracing the Deadly Path of the World's Most Precious Stones*, (Bolder CO: Westview Press, 2002), 54.

51. Donald Temple, "Sierra Leone: An Obscure Battlefield in the War on Terrorism," *The Jamestown Foundation*, http://www.jamestown.org/terrorism/news/article.php?articleid=2369857&orubttgus=1 (accessed 15 June 2007).

52. Campbell, *Blood Diamonds: Tracing the Deadly Path of the World's Most Precious Stones*, 42-43. Exporting began in 1994–1998. Additional diamonds were received illegally.

53. Truth and Reconciliation Commission of Sierra Leone, *Final Report of the Truth and Reconciliation Commission of Sierra Leone*, para 422, para 428, para 429.

54. Ibid., para 423.

55. Ibid., para 422, 428-429.

56. Ibid., para 424.

57. Ishmael Beah, *A Long Way Gone: Memoirs of a Boy Soldier*, (New York: Sarah Crichton Books, 2007), 199.

58. Ibid., 124

59. Human Rights Watch, *The Scars of Death*, http://www.hrw.org/reports/2001/children/9.htm (accessed 18 July 2007).

60. Lansana Gberie, *A Dirty War in West Africa: The RUF And the Destruction of Sierra Leone*, (Bloomington, IN: Indiana University Press, 2005), 70-71.

61. Momoh spent the last years of his life in neighboring Guinea, where he died in exile.

Chapter 2

The First Intervention: Civil War and Mercenaries, 1995–1996

After their spring 1991 offensive, the RUF controlled the diamond mines of Sierra Leone and their forces operated within 20 miles of the capital of Freetown. The Sierra Leone government under General Momoh controlled little but the old Freetown Colony. State services had collapsed and the country was in ruin. This chapter will analyze events from 1992 when a military junta seized control of the government to the 1996 Abidjan Peace Accord agreement. Faced with its own defeat, the junta turned to mercenaries in an attempt to restore its control over the country.

National Provisional Ruling Council

In April 1992, a group of disgruntled junior officers on leave in Freetown, led by Captain Valentine Strasser, overthrew President Momoh and formed a military junta known as the National Provisional Ruling Council (NPRC). The military junta consisted of about 100 soldiers displaying rocket launchers, heavy machine guns, and antiaircraft guns. The coup was popular at the time, as most Sierra Leoneans were disgruntled with the aging and ineffective APC leadership. Part of the NPRC's popularity had to do with the promise to end the war and to restore peace in Sierra Leone. The coup—marked by widespread looting—recovered over 41 billion *leones*, approximately $13.5 million, from the homes of ex-ministers and senior APC cabinet members. Within a week, the RUF, via broadcast messages, offered a cease-fire and readiness to work with the junta in the interest of peace.[1] Captain Strasser and his lieutenants, however, did not think compromise or working with the RUF was in the best interest of the government or the people of Sierra Leone.

Sierra Leone Army

One of the first goals of the NPRC was to increase the strength of the military in order to drive back RUF forces. To give the army a fresh start, the administration changed the name of the army from the RSLMF to the Sierra Leone Army (SLA). They appealed to the citizens of Sierra Leone to enlist in the army and become part of the patriotic solution to end the insurgency. Within four years, the army grew from 3,700 to over 17,000 troops. Unfortunately, many of the recruits were uneducated and unemployed, disaffected youth, some of which were under 18 years of age. Many of the recruits were also drug users and criminals. The SLA provided only the most rudimentary military training for two to six weeks before sending the new recruits to the front lines.[2]

As soldiers moved to the frontlines, volunteers came forward to help in the war effort. These voluntary cadres burgeoned into a whole new class of fighters commonly known as the "irregulars" that were comprised of vigilantes, border guards, auxiliary forces and unemployed people. These fighters were taught little more than how to fire a gun and how to respond to orders. Some of these irregulars were issued weapons and uniforms and placed on the army rolls.[3] These new soldiers had little or no discipline. Senior officers did not have control of their soldiers and many of the soldiers reverted to their old habits of drug use. Military codes of conduct existed but were not enforced. The organizational structure was lax and professionalism was nonexistent. Many of the recruits didn't even know to whom to report. As these soldiers moved into the war-affected areas, they quickly resorted to the same brutal practices of their enemies. Officers rarely took disciplinary action about complaints from civilians. If a commander was found engaging in some sort of unsavory or unscrupulous activity, the NPRC simply replaced him with another commander and sent the relieved commander back to Freetown to take another position within the military.[4]

Civilians increasingly referred to the NPRC military forces as *sobels* or "soldiers by day, rebels by night." They found a more lucrative way of making a living than working for the low wages they received. As soldiers entered villages, towns, and cities in the day, they scouted out what they could steal at night. In some cases, they would evacuate the citizens, loot the homes, and blame the RUF. When the *sobels* moved into the diamond areas, they would often work the mines and profit from smuggling.[5] Some of the officers organized groups of soldiers and local citizens to work the mines while allegedly conducting military operations for the government. In some cases, senior officers conspired with rebel groups. In exchange for a portion of the diamond harvest, they would promise not to take military action against the RUF forces. The new government estimated that as many as 20 percent of the soldiers were disloyal.[6]

The civil war consumed the NPRC leadership between 1992 and 1995. Sierra Leone's monetary situation became ever more desperate over time. The International Monetary Fund (IMF) provided loans to the new government to fund its operations. When the government was unable to repay its first installment on the loans the IMF imposed stringent guidelines as a precondition for additional loans. Strasser, the President of the NPRC, appealed to the UN for military and monetary intervention, but the UN considered the civil war an internal problem and exercised its practice of non-interference with member states.[7] Strasser desperately searched for alternatives, fully aware of the instability of his government, the ruined economy, and the approaching rebels to Freetown. Executive Outcomes (EO), a private South African mercenary firm submitted a proposal to the Strasser government and negotiations began.

The First Intervention: Executive Outcomes

In April 1995 the NPRC leader contracted with EO to conduct military operations in Sierra Leone against the RUF forces. In addition to paying EO $1.8 million per month for their military services, Strasser also entered into an agreement with Branch Energy and its subsidiary Diamond Works. EO and Diamond Works were financially linked, though the details were murky. The plan called for EO to recapture the diamond mines from the RUF, after which Diamond Works would extract the diamonds using local labor. In exchange for the effort, Diamond Works would pay the government 37.5 percent of the net profits.[8] Strasser believed that if he could return the diamond mines to government control he would be able to pay EO and have enough cash to run the government.

EO was founded in 1989 by Edben Barlow, a former South African Special Forces officer, when the elite 32d Battalion Reconnaissance Wing of the South African Defense Force was disbanded. EO recruited most of its members from the 32d Battalion, Reconnaissance Commandos, the Parachute Brigade, and the South West Africa Police Counter-Insurgency Unit or the paramilitary *Koevoet* or *Crowbar*.[9] EO maintained a permanent staff of 14 with ready access to over 2,000 recruits. Within a few weeks EO assembled a force of 500 military advisers with 3,000 highly trained combat soldiers. This capable force possessing extensive combat experience became mercenaries for the NPRC.

Strasser's government handed EO a threefold mission: to evict the RUF from areas east of Freetown, to stabilize the diamond mining area allowing Diamond Works to open the mines for the government, and to locate and destroy the RUF headquarters. In addition to the military objectives, EO was also charged with employing an information operations program to encourage Sierra Leoneans to support the decision to employ EO in the country.[10]

EO began an extensive military training program to retrain SLA soldiers. The government's intent was to bring the forces to a standard such that the SLA could operate on its own. In essence, the mission of the EO organization was to work itself out of a job. In early May 1995, EO's advance team of 30 men arrived in Sierra Leone and began evaluating, training, and restructuring the SLA. In addition to training the army, EO also began training many of the *kamajors* to operate in support of SLA infantry units.

At the same time approximately 150 EO mercenaries set about the task of securing Freetown. EO brought an Mi-8 transport helicopter, a Mi-24 Hind Russian helicopter gunship, a radio intercept system, two Boeing 727s to transport troops and supplies, and an Andover casualty-evacuation aircraft. The government provided them with SLA military uniforms, three APC's equipped with 30-mm cannons, six Land Rovers mounting anti-aircraft guns, and other weapons.[11] In 10 days of fighting EO was able to drive the RUF approximately 60 miles into the interior of the country. EO decisively overmatched the rag tag RUF units in a skillfully executed combined arms operation.[12]

EO's training program for the SLA soon bore fruit. Their superior communications equipment enabled EO and the SLA to track and monitor the whereabouts of the RUF. EO and the SLA used professional military planning and targeting methods to great effect in their assaults against the RUF, and they were able to carry out surprise attacks at night using sophisticated night-vision equipment. EO provided the SLA with the knowledge, weaponry and leadership to operate on the battlefield and gave them new found confidence to face the RUF.

In August 1995, EO troops and two retrained SLA infantry battalions supported by the Mi-24 helicopter gunship recaptured the Kono mining district from the RUF. In December 1995, EO/SLA forces retook the Sierra Rutile mine from the RUF, and by January 1996 EO/SLA forces defeated the RUF forces in the Kangari Hills, a major RUF stronghold. Although combined EO/SLA forces did not capture the RUF headquarters near Kailahun, the SLA offensive forced Sankoh to cut his losses and enter into negotiation with the government for the first time in 5 1/2 years.[13] EO conducted missions in Sierra Leone for only seven months from May 1995 till January 1996. Yet it was able to restore order to Freetown , retake the major diamond mines located in the Kono district, and force the RUF to seek peace.

Map 4. Executive Outcomes offensives, 1995-96.

1996 Elections and a New Government

The government's military success in late 1995 provided them with the breathing space to move toward elections with the aim of reestablishing civilian rule. This had been the platform upon which Strasser and the NPRC seized power in 1992. The junta set March 1996 as the date for national elections. But Strasser soon upset the process by trying to lower the mandatory age requirement of the president, as established by the constitution, from 45 years of age to one more appropriate to his age, 30. His attempts to change this policy led to his downfall and in mid January 1996 Strasser was himself overthrown in a peaceful coup by his deputy, Brigadier General Julius Bio.[14] The UN quickly threatened sanctions and EO threatened to leave the country if elections were not held by March. Bio and the NPRC succumbed to the pressure and allowed elections to take place as scheduled.[15]

Political parties and candidates conducted their campaigns in relative freedom. The ruined state of the country, however, hampered communications and enforcement of electioneering rules. Reports poured in from all over the country about local bans on rallies, indiscriminate amputations of hands and arms to prevent voting, looting and destruction of property by the RUF. Despite these many problems, on election day nearly 60 percent of the population in Sierra Leone voted. Ahmed Tejan Kabbah, the leader of the Sierra Leone People's Party (SLPP), defeated John Karefa Smart, the leader of the United National People's Party 59 to 41 percent. Kabbah was the first directly elected head of state for Sierra Leone. The military junta handed power over to Kabbah in an orderly fashion on 29 March 1996.[16]

Abidjan Peace Accord

One of Kabbah's top priorities was to bring lasting peace to Sierra Leone. Bio, in his short reign leading the junta, had persuaded Sankoh to meet him in the Ivory Coast with UN Special Envoy Berhanu Dinka, representatives of the Organization of African Unity (OAU), Great Britain, and the foreign minister of the Ivory Coast to establish a peace process. President Kabbah continued this peace process for the next eight months. They agreed on 26 of 28 negotiating points but the meetings ended when the RUF demanded withdrawal of all foreign troops, meaning EO units, and because Sankoh demanded the vice presidency. Since RUF units failed to adhere to the cease-fire during peace negotiations, the new government contracted with EO to conduct a second offensive operation to capture the RUF headquarters near Bo, the provincial capital and largest city in southern Sierra Leone. In October 1996 the combined EO/SLA/*kamajor* forces found and destroyed RUF headquarters and Sankoh admitted military defeat. Sankoh signed the Abidjan Peace Accord on 30 November 1996. The agreement included the stipulation that the EO contract would be terminated but gave Sankoh and the RUF no voice in government.[17]

The signing of the Abidjan Peace Accord between the government of Sierra Leone and the RUF promised to end Sierra Leone's 5 1/2 years of war. Sankoh promised that the RUF would adhere to the accord and both the government and RUF made a commitment to disarm, demobilize, and resettle all combatants. The war took a huge toll on its citizens and displaced over one and a half million citizens from their homes and livelihood and left more than 20,000 dead. In addition, hundreds of civilians were maimed and traumatized. At wars end, and as a promise of peace, people began migrating back to villages and urban areas seeking refuge and support.

The accord contained 28 articles and a short annex that began with the cessation of hostilities and the priority for peace.[18] A National Commission for the Consolidation of Peace (NCCP) was to be established within two weeks and would become the principle monitoring group for implementation. The NCCP was the final authority on all actions between the government and the RUF. Two other monitoring groups were also established. The first, the Joint Monitoring Group—comprised of equal representatives from the government and RUF—was to monitor the encampment, disarmament, demobilization, and reintegration process. The second, from the international community, called the Neutral Monitoring Group (NMG) was responsible for preventing breaches of the cease-fire. Once the NMG deployed to the area, EO was to leave the country within five weeks.

Articles 13 and 14 of the Agreement specifically dealt with the conduct of RUF personnel. In article 13 they were allowed to register as a political party. The RUF, although not having a clear ideology, thought this was necessary to have appropriate representation in the government. Article 14 provided RUF and the SLA fighters immunity from prosecution for acts committed by them up to the signing of the accord. This, in essence, provided them a pardon from any criminal action they committed during the revolutionary time. Article 20 established an independent National Commission on Human Rights to promote human rights education, monitor violations, and institute legal proceedings as appropriate.

The accord gave equal treatment to the RUF and the government on matters relating to war and peace, but not to issues of politics and governance. Since free democratic elections with a multi-party system were held prior to the signing of the accord, and a functioning constitution was in place, the accord accepted both as the will of the people. The RUF accepted this provision as long as it was free to establish its own political party, known as the RUFP.

The peace accord had the potential to work if both parties were serious about making it work. It contained, however, several unresolved issues that would later plague Sierra Leone. First, there was no mention of the CDF and *kamajors*. Should they remain as armed extensions of the Sierra Leonean armed forces, or should they be dissolved? Second, there was no real attempt at coming to terms with atrocities committed upon civilians. Men, women, and children were traumatized by mutilation, rape, and conscription to the war effort, but nothing was mentioned in the accord. Third, since the peace commission was composed of eight people, equally divided between the government and RUF, there was no decision-making mechanism in the event of a deadlock. Finally, the commission itself did not have a provision to replace members if they were found to be unsuitable.[19]

As early as mid-December 1996, Kabbah and Sankoh began to disagree over how to implement the Abidjan Agreement. Sankoh accused the Freetown government of violating the cease-fire because of an incident with the *kamajors*. In January the SLA intercepted a RUF radio message that indicated Sankoh had no intention of keeping the accord: the message said he signed the peace accord simply to get rid of the military pressure. From this point on, communication between the two leaders came to an end. In early March 1997, Sankoh traveled covertly to Lagos, Nigeria, to purchase weapons, but was detained by Nigerian authorities after ammunition was found in his vehicle.[20] The Abidjan Agreement would bring peace to Sierra Leone for only a short while.

Summary and Analysis of the Intervention by Executive Outcomes

As a military force EO was highly skilled and easily able to outmaneuver and outperform the RUF rebels. The insurgents had limited military strength and equipment and they did not have the training or capacity to coordinate their efforts effectively. EO forces expertly used intelligence to plan their operations and their combined use of artillery, helicopters and mobile light infantry units was something never before seen in the conflict. The most striking aspect of EO was its ability to deploy to the area within a relatively short time. On acceptance of the contract by both parties, EO provided troops and equipment in less than two weeks and began making a noticeable difference on the ground within another ten days.

EO had a well experienced chain of command, recent combat experience in South Africa, and acted aggressively to conduct combat operations throughout Sierra Leone. The average EO soldier was paid $3500 per month while top helicopter pilots and company commanders were paid $7500 per month.[21] Another strength of EO was its ability to train and to employ SLA soldiers and *kamajors* in their operations. The *kamajors* were familiar with the terrain and had favorable relations with the paramount chiefs. EO provided them with food, intelligence, training and some military planning.[22] EO established rules of conduct and rules of engagement, rehearsed operations, and depended on the soldiers to do what was necessary to complete the operation. This highly skilled force upset the balance of power and provided a victory that the NPRC could never have accomplished on their own. As Canadian General Ian Douglas, a UN negotiator, stated, "EO gave Sierra Leone a sense of stability during this critical time."[23]

Sierra Leone's decision to use EO was heavily criticized, despite its obvious military success. One of the criticisms concerned the financial relationship between EO and Diamond Works. Although the government maintained that they made separate agreements with the two firms, the comingling of objectives and financing gave the appearance of impropriety. Critics of EO argue that they were there only to plunder the economic resources of the country through their corporate partner. EO insisted that they were there to assist a failing government and provided a more cost-effective solution than multinational or internationally mandated national forces.[24] Another criticism of the use of EO was the way in which it was directed undermined the effectiveness of the government and its credibility. Instead of working for the Ministry of Defense and being accountable to the legislature, EO reported directly to President Strasser, who doubled as the Minister of Defense.[25]

The intervention by Executive Outcomes in the internal affairs of Sierra Leone had achieved its stated objectives in 1995 and 1996. EO was by far the superior military force in the country and quickly turned the military tide in favor of the government. The SLA also benefited from the training and expertise provided by EO. The NPRC junta's military success forced Sankoh and the RUF to the negotiating table and to negotiate a cease fire favorable to the government. The Abidjan Agreement of November 1996 appeared to establish a path towards political and social reunification of the country. Though the combined EO/SLA forces defeated the RUF, they did not destroy it and Sankoh remained its fanatical head. The internationally brokered peace agreement had many virtues, but its provisions were utterly dependent on the willingness of the signatories to adhere to its stipulations and assumed a common vision for the future of Sierra Leone that did not exist in 1997.

Notes

1. Lansana Gberie, *A Dirty War in West Africa: The RUF And the Destruction of Sierra Leone*, (Bloomington, IN: Indiana University Press, 2005), 70-71.
2. Ibid., 76.
3. Truth and Reconciliation Commission of Sierra Leone, *Final Report of the Truth and Reconciliation Commission of Sierra Leone*, Chapter 3, para 320, http://trcsierraleone.org/drwebsite/publish/v3a-c1.shtml, (accessed 10 June 2007).
4. Ibid.
5. William Shawcross, "Sierra Leone Defies Fear and Heads for the Polls," *International Herald Tribune*, 15 March 1996, http://www.iht.com/articles/1996/03/15/edshaw.t.php (accessed 10 June 2007).
6. Gberie, *A Dirty War in West Africa: The RUF And the Destruction of Sierra Leone*, 91.
7. David Keen, *Conflict and Collusion in Sierra Leone*, (New York: Palgrave Publishers, 2005), 91-92.
8. John L. Hirsch, *Sierra Leone: Diamonds and the Struggle for Democracy*, (Boulder, CO: Lynne Rienner Publishers, 2001), 39.
9. William Bowles, "Executive Outcomes: Tony Blair's Pet Bulldog? The Curious Case of Tim Spicer," posted 18 August 2004, http://www.williambowles.info/ini/ini-0266.html (accessed on 11 July 2007).
10. Michael van Maanen, "Saving the Sum of Things for Pay: Executive Outcomes in Sierra Leone," *Incite: Journal of Political Opinion and Analysis*, http://www.geocities.com/CollegePark/Square/6130/archive.htm (accessed 11 July 2007).
11. Ibid., 94.
12. Gberie, *A Dirty War in West Africa: The RUF And the Destruction of Sierra Leone*, 92-93.
13. Hirsch, *Sierra Leone: Diamonds and the Struggle for Democracy*, 39.
14. In a council meeting, after Strasser made a speech, Bio said he would not support him. Bio pulled out a pistol and pointed it at Strasser's head. A struggle ensued but was quickly contained and handcuffs were placed on Strasser. Strasser was then flown out of the country to neighboring Guinea, where Joseph Momoh was also a refugee. The whole operation took less than five minutes. Julius Bio maintained a statesmanlike demeanor in the midst of personal crisis. The RUF had captured his two sisters and brother-in-law in 1991. His sisters were subjected to continual sexual violence and were forced to do domestic chores. If they tried to escape, whoever was left would be killed. Putting nation above self, he shook hands with Sankoh during the Abidjan Peace Accord. See Truth and Reconciliation Commission of Sierra Leone, *Final Report of the Truth and Reconciliation Commission of Sierra Leone*, Chapter 3, para 618, http://trcsierraleone.org/drwebsite/publish/v3a-c1.shtml (accessed 6 July 2007).

15. van Maanen, "Saving the Sum of Things for Pay: Executive Outcomes in Sierra Leone."

16. Sierra Leone Web, "Sierra Leone News Archive, 29 March 1996," http://www.sierra-leone.org/slnews0396.html (accessed 8 July 2007).

17. Tom Cooper and Court Chick, "Western and Northern Africa Database–Sierra Leone 1990-2002," *Air Combat Information Group Journal*, (5 August 2004), http://www.acig.org/artman/publish/article_462.shtml (accessed 19 June 2007).

18. "The Abidjan Peace Accord," 30 November 1996, *Peace Agreement between the Government of the Republic of Sierra Leone and the Revolutionary United Front of Sierra Leone (RUF/SL)*, http://www.sc-sl.org/abidjanaccord.html (accessed 10 July 2007).

19. The problems of the peace accord are part of the written reflections by Yusuf Bangura, "Reflections on the Abidjan Peace Accord," *Africa Development*, vol. XXII, Numbers 3 & 4, 1997, Council for the Development of Social Science Research in Africa, http://www.codesria.org/Links/Publications/ad_contents/3&4_1997.htm (accessed 10 July 2007).

20. Hirsch, *Sierra Leone: Diamonds and the Struggle for Democracy*, 54-55.

21. Herbert M. Howe, "Private Security Forces and African Stability: The Case of Executive Outcomes," *The Journal of Modern African Studies*, Vol 36, No. 2, (June 1998), 307-331, http://www.jstor.org/sici?sici=0022-278X(199806)36%3A2%3C307%3APSFAAS%3E2.0.CO%3B2-4 (accessed 18 May 07).

22. Ibid.

23. Ibid.

24. van Maanen, "Saving the Sum of Things for Pay: Executive Outcomes in Sierra Leone."

25. Howe, "Private Security Forces and African Stability: The Case of Executive Outcomes," 307-331.

Chapter 3

The Second Intervention: The Economic Community of West African States, 1995–2000

By late 1996 Executive Outcomes mercenaries, hired in 1995 by the Strasser government, had driven the RUF far into the countryside and restored the government's power over much of the country. This operation succeeded in bringing the RUF to the bargaining table with the government holding the stronger hand. The Abidjan Agreement of November 1996 was designed to bring peace to Sierra Leone and gave the RUF no voice in the Kabbah government which had been elected in March of that year. By mid 1997, however, civil war returned to Sierra Leone and a second round of external military interventions was launched by some of Sierra Leone's West African neighbors. This chapter will focus on the developments between 1997 and the controversial Lome Peace Agreement of July 1999. It will specifically look at the intervention by the Economic Community of West African States (ECOWAS) and their military force known as the Military Observer Group or ECOMOG.

Prelude to Intervention: ECOMOG, Sierra Leone, and Liberia

ECOMOG, the military arm of the thirteen West African states making up ECOWAS, actually conducted its first operations in Sierra Leone in August 1990 when it intervened in the Liberian civil war to assist the Liberian government of Sergeant Samuel Doe in defeating the rebel force led by Charles Taylor. Ghana, Guinea, Sierra Leone, Gambian and Nigeria contributed troops, with the bulk of the forces and support being provided by Nigeria. ECOMOG forces first deployed into Sierra Leone in May 1992. It attempted to seal the border with Liberia, to cut off one of Charles Taylor's Liberian rebels' source of supplies and men. ECOMOG used the Lungi airport north of Freetown as their supply base, and ECOMOG troops were stationed at key places in the country to guard their supply lines to the south. They soon became involved in assisting the Sierra Leone government in its battle with RUF forces being supported from Liberia. Their situation in Sierra Leone became tenuous in May 1997 when the Kabbah government, which was supported by Nigeria, was overthrown and ECOMOG suddenly found itself in the midst of a country whose new government demanded their exit.

Armed Forces Revolutionary Council

As the last of the EO mercenaries departed Freetown on 7 February 1997 in accordance with the Abidjan Agreement, the Sierra Leone Army assumed responsibility for law and order in the country. Trying to pull the country together soon proved tougher for the Kabbah government than expected. Fighting continued in the hinterland between varying SLA/CDF units and RUF factions, and urban strife continued in Freetown. In their quest to support rebels fighting Charles Taylor in Liberia to the south, ECOMOG troops were bound up in the fighting between the Sierra Leone government and RUF units in the southern and eastern parts of the country. The lack of law and order throughout the countryside after years of fighting and chaos made it hard for the government to meet the high expectations of Sierra Leoneans and the international community. Compounding the problem was the downsizing of the military, lack of funds to run government programs, pressure from the IMF to cut government spending, continued loss of jobs, rising prices, and declining incomes. Within a month, Sierra Leone descended again into chaos.

In May 1997, a group of disaffected soldiers arrested several senior officers, blasted open Pademba Road Prison in Freetown releasing more than 600 convicts, and supplied them with arms. This force then attacked the State House and named 33-year old Major Johnny Paul Koroma—in Pademba Road Prison on treason charges—as ruler of the self-proclaimed Armed Forces Revolutionary Council (AFRC).[1] Koroma immediately suspended the constitution, banned demonstrations, shutdown newspapers and closed radio stations, abolished all political parties, and placed many of his soldiers in leadership positions. President Kabbah and his government went into exile into neighboring Guinea on 26 May 1997.

To justify the AFRC coup, Koroma cited corruption in the government, erosion of state sovereignty, dependence on foreign nations for finances, and failure of the government to adequately address tensions between the SLA and the *kamajors*. In a startling move to end the fighting between the government and the RUF, Koroma invited the leadership of the RUF to join the AFRC, which they promptly did. Although Sankoh was being detained by Nigeria, Koroma offered him the vice-chairmanship of the new junta government and he accepted. Sankoh ordered his RUF fighters into Freetown to join the soldiers' revolt.[2] US Marines evacuated some 1,200 foreign nationals and aid workers from the Mammy Yoko Hotel in Freetown with the assistance of a small ECOMOG detachment in the waning days of May and early June.[3] In the chaos, some ECOMOG troops in Freetown were taken prisoner by the AFRC/RUF forces.[4]

The rule of the joint AFRC/RUF coup was characterized by complete chaos and barbarism. Every state service, to include schools, banks, health clinics, commercial services, and government offices ceased to function. The soldiers of the AFRC/RUF alliance intimidated the business owners, government ministers, diplomats, humanitarian aid workers, and journalists of Freetown by confiscating vehicles, merchandize, and money.[5] Law and order was replaced by rape, torture, looting, and murder. The country's roads and ferry networks, in bad shape before the war, suffered even more damage as the rebellion continued. In many places outside Freetown, villages were accessible only by helicopter due to poor road conditions and ambushes.

Regional West African Community Response

ECOWAS, African regional organizations and the international community roundly condemned the coup. ECOMOG forces in Sierra Leone continued to operate along the border with Liberia but after their initial attempts in late May, held off from attempting to overthrow the AFRC/RUF government. They also agreed on a three-phase strategy to include dialogue, sanctions, and the use military force. During the opening phase, a group of five international members met directly with representatives of the AFRC leadership to demand that the new junta return, peacefully, power to the Kabbah government. ECOWAS held regional meetings at Abidjan, Ivory Coast in July 1997 and at Conakry, Guinea in October with delegations representing Koroma and the AFRC/RUF junta. Both groups signed the Conakry Peace Plan on 23 October 1997. Koroma agreed to return to power the Kabbah government no later than April 1998 in exchange for immunity for him, his followers, and the release of the RUF leader, Foday Sankoh from Nigeria. The key sections of the agreement stated:

> 5. To that end, the Committee of Five and the representatives of Major Johnny Paul Koroma adopted an ECOWAS peace plan for Sierra Leone and a timetable for its implementation over a six-month period with effect from 23 October 1997.
>
> 6. It is recognized that Corporal Foday Sankoh, as a leader of the Revolutionary United Front (RUF), could continue to play an active role and participate in the peace process. In the spirit of the Abidjan Accord and in the context of this agreement,

Corporal Sankoh is expected to return to his country to make his contribution to the peace process.

7. The ECOWAS peace plan for Sierra Leone provides for:

a. The reinstatement of the legitimate Government of President Tejan Kabbah within a period of six months;

b. The immediate cessation of hostilities;

c. Cooperation of the junta with ECOMOG in order to enforce the sanctions peacefully;

d. Disarmament, demobilization and reintegration of combatants;

e. Provision of humanitarian assistance;

f. Return of refugees and displaced persons;

g. Immunities and guarantees to the leaders of the coup d'état of 25 May 1997;

h. Modalities for broadening the power base in Sierra Leone.[6]

As Koroma contemplated the effect of this agreement on his future power, he changed his mind and declared that he would remain in power for another two to four years, claiming that the AFRC needed this time to restore normalcy to Sierra Leone. As this was unacceptable to ECOWAS, it began the second phase of its strategy—economic sanctions—into effect. The international community isolated Sierra Leone by severing international ties, enforcing an embargo on international trade, and placing additional new sanctions on the AFRC leadership. The strategy of dialogue and sanctions had little effect on the AFRC. By November 1997 it had become clear that armed intervention was the only way to remove the AFRC junta and to restore the elected government of Sierra Leone.[7] ECOWAS deployed ECOMOG soldiers to intervene in Sierra Leone in early 1998 to restore the democratic government.

In February 1998, ECOMOG soldiers comprised mostly of Nigerian soldiers launched Operation SANDSTORM, an offensive to restore the Kabbah government to power. As others would do later, ECOMOG used the Lungi airport across the bay and north of Freetown where the Kabbah government in exile was still in control. ECOMOG forces then moved to the south around the Sierra Leone River estuary that is east of the Freetown peninsula and established a forward base near the town of Hastings about twenty miles south of the city of Freetown. A majority of the participating forces were airlifted to old Hastings airfield. The first phase of the operation, aimed at the capture of the capital of Freetown and the deposing of the AFRC junta under Koroma in Freetown, was launched on 2 February 1998 and was named Operation TIGERHEAD. The three-pronged attack on the city was conducted with three Nigerian infantry battalions each assisted by small ad hoc contingents of ex-policeman, military officers and university students who were loyal to the Sierra Leone government in exile. One battalion attacked north into the eastern part of Freetown along the road from Jui through Calaba Town. The second attacked north into the center of Freetown along the peninsular road coming from Waterloo to Hastings, and the third battalion attacked the western part of Freetown through the Regent–Grafton axis and headed towards the old British settlement of Wilberforce.[8]

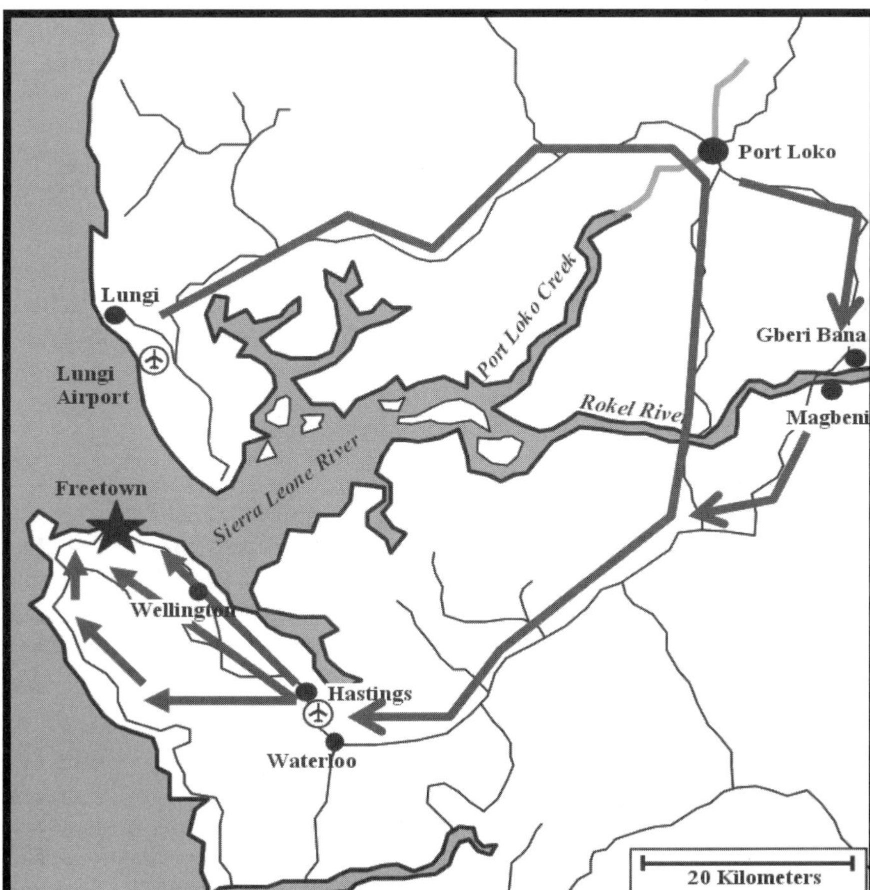

Map 5. ECOMOG operations near Freetown, 1998.

The ECOMOG attack got off to a slow start due to due to strong resistance from the AFRC and RUF on all three of its routes. ECOMOG forces encountered AFRC fortifications including well placed land mines. In addition, Nigerian forces reported that AFRC positions were initially defended by artillery support from Ukrainian mercenaries. ECOMOG leaders spent ten days attacking AFRC positions before getting in place to assault the city. ECOMOG units successfully broke into Freetown on 12–13 February 1998.[9]

In a measure that might have lessened resistance in the city, ECOMOG forces allowed AFRC and RUF fighters to flee Freetown by ground and sea. Civilians in Freetown were once again subjected to an orgy of atrocities by fleeing AFRC and RUF fighters. ECOMOG later may have regretted the decision to allow safe passage out of Freetown because many AFRC and RUF forces reconstituted themselves less than a month later. The Government of President Kabbah was reinstated in a ceremony at the State House on 10 March 1998 with great fanfare. ECOMOG appeared to have quickly achieved a stunning success.[10]

As ECOMOG moved beyond the outlying areas of Freetown and into the hinterland, however, it met with only marginal success. ECOMOG personnel were able to liberate the cities of Masiaka, Makeni, and Kabala which lie in a belt around Freetown in the center west part of the country. But the further north or east from Freetown that ECOMOG forces traveled, RUF forces again offered stiff resistance. Due to poor road conditions and a lack of aircraft, logistical units were unable to keep the force in supplies and ammunition.[11] As ECOMOG's offensive stalled, its units took up defensive positions.

Prior to the official return of President Kabbah on 10 March 1998, the citizens of Freetown carried out numerous executions of collaborators and perpetrators of AFRC/RUF atrocities. This short period was marked by mob justice, vigilantes, and basic civil disorder. Civilians made numerous reports of ECOMOG soldiers using brutality and excessive force to control the situation.[12] Until a task force was established to provide basic police action, ECOMOG soldiers did not know who the enemies among the citizens were. Eventually Freetown was brought under control and Kabbah arrived to tend to matters of state.

Once restored to the presidency by ECOMOG units, President Kabbah immediately took action to hold the AFRC soldiers responsible for their rebellion. Many of the soldiers who perpetrated the coup were confined to

Pedemba Road Prison, from where many of them had been earlier released. Kabbah also demobilized the entire army and held courts-martial for the coup leaders. Following the courts-martial, twenty-four AFRC military officers were executed.[13] RUF leader and AFRC co-leader Foday Sankoh was arrested in Nigeria, returned to Sierra Leone, tried, found guilty, and sentenced to death. His sentence was not immediately carried out.

On 13 July 1998, the UN Security Council—as requested in the Conakry Agreement—established the United Nations Observer Mission to Sierra Leone (UNOMSIL) with 70 unarmed military observers and 15 medical personnel. Brigadier-General Subhash C. Joshi of India served as the Chief Military Observer under the Chief of Mission, Mr. Francis G. Okelo from Uganda.[14] Paragraph six of UN Security Council Resolution 1181 tasked UNOMSIL to:

> a. Monitor the military and security situation in the country as a whole, as security conditions permit, and to provide the Special Representative of the Secretary-General with regular information thereon in particular with a view to determining when conditions were sufficiently secure to allow subsequent deployments of military observers beyond the first phase;
>
> b. Monitor the disarmament and demobilization of former combatants concentrated in secure areas of the country, including monitoring of the role of the Military Observer Group (ECOMOG) of the Economic Community of West African States (ECOWAS) in the provision of security and in the collection and destruction of arms in those secure areas;
>
> c. Assist in monitoring respect for international humanitarian law, including at disarmament and demobilization sites, where security conditions permit;
>
> d. Monitor the voluntary disarmament and demobilization of members of the Civil Defence Forces (CDF), as security conditions permit.[15]

The resolution also requested ECOMOG to provide security for the unarmed UNOMSIL force.

The executions of some of their leaders by the Kabbah government after the Conakry Agreement, and the death sentence imposed on Sankoh in absentia infuriated the AFRC/RUF members and intensified their drive for revenge.[16] With this as a motivation, the AFRC/RUF regrouped and remobilized their forces and trained new recruits. They sent hundreds of their combatants to Gbatala, Liberia for training led by mercenaries from Ukraine, Burkina, Nigeria, Libya, and South Africa. In a return to their previous practices, they captured civilians and children, forcing them to participate in the revolutionary movement. As Amnesty International reported:

> Since their removal from power, the AFRC and RUF have wreaked a campaign of terror against unarmed civilians and human rights abuses have reached unprecedented levels. Several thousand civilians have been brutally killed or mutilated. Hundreds of others have been abducted from their villages and forced to join the revolutionary movement.[17]

AFRC/RUF devised a bold plan to recapture Freetown. First, they acquired enough recruits so that when they approached Freetown the sheer number of participants would overwhelm the weak government forces. Second, the AFRC/RUF planned to use women and children to shield their fighters during the fighting around Freetown. The rebels knew that using civilians as shields would catch ECOMOG soldiers off guard and put them in the untenable military situation of being peacekeepers forced to fire upon civilians.[18]

The RUF deputy commander Sam Bockarie (alias Mosquito) planned the attack to retake Freetown and to free Sankoh from prison in one stroke. He had many of his rebel forces infiltrate the city prior to his planned attack. In January 1999, a 10,000 person mob marched toward Freetown; it was a mixture of civilians and RUF/SLA combatants disguised as civilians.[19] Bockarie called the attack Operation NO LIVING THING. They were able to quickly find unmanned entry points into the city. Undermanned and less than fully professional ECOMOG forces were in disarray and unable to hold the entry points. For 2 weeks the AFRC/RUF mobs rampaged throughout the city in an orgy of looting, amputations, rape and killing. Sadly, ECOMOG units proved to be equally ruthless, capturing and killing anyone they thought was connected with the RUF. Some ECOMOG soldiers also took part in the atrocities against civilians caught up in the chaos. The tiny UNOMSIL force departed the country in haste in January 1999 when it became clear that there was no reconciliation to observe and that their lives were in danger.[20]

President Kabbah was evacuated to the Lungi airport by the ECOMOG to ensure his safety. While at Lungi, Kabbah called the Nigerian leader, General Abdulsalami Abubakar, to request additional assistance.[21] General Abubaker immediately deployed several additional battalions of soldiers and replaced the ineffectual ECOMOG commander, General Shelpidi, with General Khobe. Khobe was a general who knew the terrain and was familiar with urban operations. Within 10 days of their arrival the new ECOMOG battalions were on the offensive against the AFRC/RUF attackers. The fighting was unusually intense by the standards of previous conflicts in Sierra Leone when weaker units melted away after brief firefights. Every street had to be fought for and both sides suffered heavy casualties. As the AFRC/RUF forces were gradually forced out of Freetown they turned the battle into an orgy of looting, destruction, abduction, rapes, and killings.[22]

After three weeks of fighting Freetown was restored to order by ECOMOG. An estimated 10,000 people had been killed, including cabinet members, journalists, and lawyers. Before the rebels were driven out of the area, they burned large parts of the city. Over 150,000 people were now homeless and an additional 600,000 sought asylum in neighboring countries. As the rebels departed the city, they abducted over 3,000 women and children.[23]

While ECOMOG units were liberating Freetown, CDF militias took up the offensive against RUF units throughout the country. Armed with weapons supplied by Nigeria, they were able to take control of several areas controlled by the RUF. Although the CDF was fighting for the government to end RUF atrocities, its members also looted villages and killed civilians suspected of aiding the rebels.[24] Their tactics became as ruthless as those of the RUF.

After the Nigerian led ECOMOG force cleared Freetown of the AFRC/RUF rebels it halted its operations; they were not prepared for and did not have a mandate to extend their operations beyond restoration of the Kabbah government in Freetown. The government of Nigeria was also anxious to pull away from ECOMOG and begin the process of disengaging its troops from Sierra Leone. Because of the immense civilian suffering and the likelihood of more if ECOMOG troops pulled out of Sierra Leone without a peace deal of some kind, the international community again intervened to mediate negotiations between the government and rebels. The United Nations, the United States, Britain, and the OAU sent representatives to Lome, the capitol of Togo, to work out a possible solution to the crisis in Sierra Leone. The now familiar pattern of partial military success by one side, followed by some sort of brokered peace returned.

In July 1999, the RUF, AFRC, and President Kabbah reached a controversial peace agreement, known as the Lome Peace Agreement (see Appendix B for key excerpts from the Lome Agreement), putting in place arrangements for a shared government. President Clinton and the US government played a key role in pressuring Kabbah to accept a unity government that included RUF participation, which Kabbah was not inclined to do on his own. Clinton sent Jesse Jackson as a US special envoy to the peace negotiations. As part of the agreement, Sankoh was pardoned of treason, granted the status of vice president which had been denied him by the Abidjan Agreement three years earlier, and made chairman of a commission with powers to regulate the country's diamonds. The Lome agreement granted amnesty to Koroma and his AFRC troops. In addition, the RUF was allowed to form yet another political party, known as the Revolutionary United Front Party (RUFP), and hold elected office. The RUFP also received one senior and three other ministry positions as well as four deputy minister posts.[25]

In return for recognition as a legitimate political party and partner in the government, the RUF was required to dissolve its military forces through a process of disarmament, demobilization, and reintegration (DDR). This process would be monitored by a neutral force provided by the United Nations, representatives of the government, as well as RUF, SLA, and CDF units themselves. ECOMOG forces were to remain in place until the UN force deployed to the country, though some of its troops would become part of the new United Nations Assistance Mission in Sierra Leone (UNAMSIL). Lome also called for a new Truth and Reconciliation Commission as well as a Special Court to deal with human rights violations. The Lome Peace Agreement was not very popular with the citizens of Sierra Leone because Foday Sankoh and other RUF leaders who were offered seats in the new government were exempt from prosecution by the Special Court for their crimes against humanity.[26] The UN Security Council passed Resolution 1270 on 22 October 1999 authorizing a new UN force to be deployed to Sierra Leone by January 2000 (discussed in the next chapter). Nigerian and ECOMOG forces were withdrawn from Sierra Leone in March and April 2000, and formally turned over responsibility to the new UN force on 4 May 2000.

Analysis of ECOMOG Interventions

The intervention by ECOMOG was an attempt by regional African nations to solve their own internal problems. In that regard, it was seen as an important milestone on the maturation of African states as controlling their own destiny free of non-regional and mercenary actors. To its credit, ECOMOG was endorsed not only by the United Nations, but by Africans themselves. Under the umbrella of ECOWAS, the member nations included Benin, Burkina Faso, Cape Verde, Côte d'Ivoire, Gambia, Ghana, Guinea, Guinea-Bissau, Liberia, Mali, Niger, Nigeria, Senegal, Sierra Leone, and Togo. Although the concept was marred by political and military shortcomings, ECOMOG was a promising alternative to the UN peacekeeping missions. The experience, training, and resources of its military forces were initially seen as a model for Africa's security system. Its record in Sierra Leone was mixed.

ECOMOG's shortcomings became most evident when it failed to halt the advance of resurgent rebel forces into Freetown in January 1999. ECOMOG's leaders had sufficient intelligence dating back to November 1998 that indicated the AFRC and RUF were planning an attack on the city, but ECOMOG's leaders disregarded the indicators. This failure left Freetown largely defenseless in January 1999 and allowed the rebel force to bring havoc upon the citizens. Poor leadership by General Shelpidi was at the root of the problem.[27]

Second, ECOMOG units were plagued by poor morale and poor discipline. Many of the soldiers deployed to Freetown in January 1998 were the same soldiers who had served in Liberia as part of the ECOWAS intervention in that war-torn country. Rank and file soldiers watched officers go home on leave, but they were not allowed the same privilege. Additionally, many of the soldiers were not paid on a regular basis leading to very poor morale, a reluctance to perform dangerous military tasks, and the use of extortion, corruption and diamond smuggling to supplement their incomes. ECOMOG soldiers also showed the same tendency to commit atrocities against the civilian population as did the AFRC/RUF rebels they were fighting.

Third, the multinational ECOMOG contingent was plagued by poor command and control. The force package sent to Sierra Leone included soldiers from Mali, Guinea, Nigeria, and Ghana. Nigeria was the largest and strongest state in ECOWAS and since it contributed the bulk of forces to ECOMOG, it commanded the overall mission. Other national contingents were reluctant to submit to Nigerian command, and often conducted their own operations under their own commanders. To make matters worse, the commander of ECOMOG, Major General Maxwell Khobe, was widely suspected of collaborating with the RUF. He was allegedly to have taken a $10 million diamond bribe from the RUF in exchange for small arms and light weapons. Other ECOMOG military commanders were suspected of complicity in the scheme.[28] This alleged corruption made the already tenuous command and control situation even more problematic. In addition, several states within the ECOWAS pledged to support the military mission but failed to deliver on their pledges.

Fourth, ECOMOG units suffered from a variety of operational and tactical military weaknesses. Most ECOMOG troops were unfamiliar with the terrain of Sierra Leone and with jungle warfare. Trained to fight conventional battles, they were vulnerable to ambushes, raids, and surprise attacks. They often relied on the *kamajors* to conduct operations in the hinterlands, which led the *kamajors* to wonder why ECOMOG was needed at all.[29] During most of the eighteen month deployment, ECOMOG had only enough soldiers to control Freetown. This inadequacy left the rest of the land in the hands of the rebels. Further, ECOMOG had limited air and sea capability. The lack of transportation severely limited their mobility over Sierra Leone's almost non-existent road network. This lack of capacity caused immense logistical problems as ECOMOG units attempted to operate away from their supply bases in Freetown.

Fifth, funding for the operations was also a problem. The war was costing a million dollars a day and ECOWAS did not have the resources to fund it.[30] Nigeria absorbed most of the funding shortfall, but this financial drain eventually led to its departure. ECOMOG was simply not financially prepared to support military intervention over a long period of time.

Finally, like the Sierra Leone government and Executive Outcomes before it, ECOMOG failed to devote enough effort to develop and train new security forces for Sierra Leone to provide law and order once external military forces left the country. Many of the newly trained soldiers turned against the Nigerians after being sent to the front.[31]

Summary

Like the intervention by mercenaries from Executive Outcomes in 1995 and 1996, the intervention in Sierra Leone by ECOMOG forces between 1997 and 1999 brought a fragile peace to the country. The UN observer mission, UNOMSIL, was a complete failure in January 1999, not so much because of its own weaknesses, but because there was simply no peace to observe. Despite the pious wording of the Conakry Communique, the parties to the agreement were clearly not ready to make peace with one another. Though plagued by many military weaknesses of its own, ECOMOG was sufficiently powerful enough to restore the Kabbah government to power and enable it to negotiate with the RUF rebels. But ECOMOG's limited mandate and military weaknesses left the RUF in control of much of the eastern and southern parts of Sierra Leone. Kabbah was therefore forced to make considerable concessions to the RUF in the Lome Agreement of July 1999 in return for an end to the fighting.

The Lome Agreement contained various mechanisms for rebuilding the country, reconciling its political parties, and disarming the various armed factions in the country. It was based on the assumption that the key political and military leaders in Sierra Leone were prepared to set aside their long standing differences and work together. As was the case with the November 1996 Abidjan Peace Agreement and the October 1997 Conakry Peace Agreement, the Lome Agreement would also fail to work, leading to a third wave of external military intervention in Sierra Leone. That intervention would itself generate the need for a brief, fourth intervention.

Notes

1. Koroma was in prison since August for an attempted coup on the elected government. This coup was part of the "*sobel*" element in the army, and Koroma's record as an officer "on the take" was well established.
2. Conciliation Resources, "Profiles–Sierra Leone," http://www.c-r.org/our-work/accord/sierra-leone/profiles.php (accessed 8 August 2007).
3. CNN Interactive, "Sierra Leone Fighting Eases, Allowing More Evacuations–3 June 1997," Cable News Network, http://www.cnn.com/WORLD/9706/03/sierra.leone (accessed 8 August 2007). See also Kwaku Nuarmah and William Zartman, "Intervention in Sierra Leone," in *Military Intervention: Cases in Context for the Twenty-First Century*, William J. Lahneman (New York: Rowmann and Littlefield, 2004), 133-150.
4. Nuarmah and Zartman, "Intervention in Sierra Leone."
5. Earl Conteh-Morgan and Mac Dixon-Fyle, *Sierra Leone at the End of the Twentieth Century*, (New York: Peter Lang Publishing, Inc, 1999), 143.

6. United States Institute of Peace, "Economic Community of West African States six-month peace plan for Sierra Leone (23 October 1997-22 April 1998), 23 October 1997," Peace Agreements Digital Collection: Sierra Leone, http://www.usip.org/library/pa/sl/sl_ecowas_10231997.html (accessed 3 August 2007).

7. Truth and Reconciliation Commission of Sierra Leone, *Final Report of the Truth and Reconciliation Commission of Sierra Leone*, Chapter 3, sections 850-863, http://trcsierraleone.org/drwebsite/publish/v3a-c1.shtml (accessed 3 August 2007). This section contains the three strategies.

8. Ibid.

9. Ibid.

10. Ibid.

11. Ibid., sections 880-886.

12. Ibid., sections 887-889.

13. Ibid., section 959.

14. United Nations Department of Peacekeeping Operations, "Sierra Leone–UNOMSIL," The United Nations, http://www.un.org/Depts/DPKO/Missions/unomsil/UnomsilF.html (accessed 3 August 2007).

15. Ibid.

16. Truth and Reconciliation Commission of Sierra Leone, *Final Report of the Truth and Reconciliation Commission of Sierra Leone*, Chapter 3, section 986.

17. Amnesty International, "Sierra Leone: 1998–A Year of Atrocities Against Civilians," November 1998, http://web.amnesty.org/library/Index/engAFR510221998 (accessed 3 August 2007).

18. Truth and Reconciliation Commission of Sierra Leone, *Final Report of the Truth and Reconciliation Commission of Sierra Leone*, Chapter 3, sections 981-983.

19. Ibid., section 1007.

20. Nuarmah and Zartman, "Intervention in Sierra Leone," 133-150. The UNOMSIL mission was officially ended by the UN in October 1999 when it was replaced by the new UNAMSIL force.

21. Ibid., para 1028.

22. Ibid.

23. David Pratt, MP, *Sierra Leone: The Forgotten Crisis*, report to Canadian Minister of Foreign Affairs, Lloyd Axworthy, PC, MP, 23 April 1999.

24. Greg Campbell, *Blood Diamonds: Tracing the Deadly Path of the World's Most Precious Stones*, (Bolder CO: Westview Press, 2002), 85-86.

25. David Keen, *Conflict and Collusion in Sierra Leone*, (New York: Palgrave Publishers, 2005), 250-252.

26. Kwaku Nuarmah and William Zartman, "Case Study: Intervention in Sierra Leone," Center for International and Security Studies at Maryland (CISSM), http://www.cissm.umd.edu/papers/files/sera_leone.pdf (accessed 3 August 2007).

27. Ibrahim Abdullah, ed., *Between Democracy and Terror,* (Oxford: African Books Collection, 2004), 231-237.

28. Dena Montague, "The Business of War and the Prospects for Peace in Sierra Leone," *The Brown Journal of World Affairs*, (Spring 2002, Volume IX, Issue 1), http://www.worldpolicy.org/projects/arms/news/brown.pdf (accessed 8 August 2007).

29. Comfort Ero, "ECOMOG: A model for Africa?" *Institute for Security Studies Monograph Series*, no. 46 (February 2000) http://www.iss.co.za/Pubs/Monographs/No46/Ecomog.html (accessed 10 August 2007).

30. Adekeye Adebajo, "Building Peace in West Africa: Liberia, Sierra Leone, and Guinea-Bissau," *African Studies Quarterly–Online Journal of African Studies*, http://www.africa.ufl.edu/asq/v7/v7i4a11.htm (accessed 10 August 2007).

31. David Leatherwood, *The Hazards of Strange Bedfellows: The United States, Nigeria, and Peacekeeping in West Africa* (Washington DC: National War College, 2000), http://www.ndu.edu/library/n2/n01LeatherwoodHazards.doc (accessed 3 August 2007).

Chapter 4

The Third and Fourth Interventions: United Nations and British Forces, 1999–2002

The intervention by Executive Outcomes mercenaries in 1995 and 1996, and the intervention by troops from the ECOWAS countries between 1997 and 1999 into Sierra Leone's civil wars were at best only partially successful. By returning the military balance of power back to the government side, each intervention led to a brokered peace. But since the RUF rebels were never decisively defeated, RUF leaders and RUF political parties were granted significant concessions in those peace agreements. In both cases, the government and regional powers were unable to turn military success into lasting political success and civil war soon returned. In late 1999 the world hoped that the Lome Agreement and UN intervention would bring lasting peace to Sierra Leone. This chapter will analyze the third and fourth external interventions, this time led by the United Nations and Great Britain, as they attempted to bring order to Sierra Leone.

United Nations Assistance Mission in Sierra Leone

Just over a year after the UNOMSIL effort ignominiously departed Freetown in complete failure, the UN again intervened in Sierra Leone. This time, the Lome Agreement seemed to hold out real promise for peace between the Kabbah government and the defeated RUF forces. Having learned that a tiny observer force was of little use, the UN in 1999 was determined to learn from its mistakes. To assist with implementation of the July Lome Peace Agreement, the United Nations passed Resolution 1270 on 22 October 1999. Resolution 1270 authorized the creation a new UN force known as the United Nations Assistance Mission in Sierra Leone (UNAMSIL), a peacekeeping and monitoring force of 210 observers and 6,000 military personnel. Unlike the UNOMSIL mission that was strictly an observer force, UNAMSIL possessed significant military power. UN Security Council ordered UNAMSIL to assist with the Disarmament, Demobilization, and Reintegration (DDR) process conducted in accordance with the terms of the Lome Agreement. Its stated mission was:

> (a) To cooperate with the Government of Sierra Leone and the other parties to the Peace Agreement in the implementation of the Agreement;

> (b) To assist the Government of Sierra Leone in the implementation of the disarmament, demobilization and reintegration plan;
>
> (c) To that end, to establish a presence at key locations throughout the territory of Sierra Leone, including at disarmament/reception centres and demobilization centres;
>
> (d) To ensure the security and freedom of movement of United Nations personnel;
>
> (e) To monitor adherence to the cease-fire in accordance with the cease-fire agreement of 18 May 1999 (S/1999/585, annex) through the structures provided for therein;
>
> (f) To encourage the parties to create confidence-building mechanisms and support their functioning;
>
> (g) To facilitate the delivery of humanitarian assistance;
>
> (h) To support the operations of United Nations civilian officials, including the Special Representative of the Secretary-General and his staff, human rights officers and civil affairs officers;
>
> (i) To provide support, as requested, to the elections, which are to be held in accordance with the present constitution of Sierra Leone.[1]

Although Resolution 1270 was passed under Chapter VII (Peace Enforcement) of the UN Charter which authorizes the use of force, paragraph 14 of the Resolution limited UNAMSIL's use of force to "ensuring the security and freedom of movement of its personnel and within its capabilities and areas of deployment, to afford protection to civilians under imminent threat of physical violence taking into account the responsibilities of the Government of Sierra Leone and ECOMOG."[2] The UN Secretary General Kofi Annan and others clearly hoped that ECOMOG forces in Sierra Leone would provide security and that UNAMSIL would inherit a relatively peaceful situation once it arrived and deployed. As paragraph 11 of UN Resolution 1270 stated, the UN:

> Commends the readiness of ECOMOG to continue to provide security for the areas where it is currently located, in particular around Freetown and Lungi, to provide protection for the Government of Sierra Leone, to conduct other operations in accordance with their mandate to ensure the implementation of the Peace Agreement, and to initiate and proceed with disarma-

ment and demobilization in conjunction and full coordination with UNAMSIL.[3]

As the resolution was being debated and nations were being asked to contribute to UNAMSIL, the newly elected president of Nigeria, Olusegun Obasanjo, announced his decision to quickly withdraw the substantial Nigerian contingent of ECOMOG.[4] Annan eventually reached an agreement with President Obasanjo to keep some of the ECOMOG forces in Sierra Leone until UNAMSIL was in place. Nigeria also agreed to become part of UNAMSIL, with funding for the mission provided by the United Nations. But Nigeria would not lead the new UN force because the United Nations wanted UNAMSIL to be seen as a neutral force in contrast to the Nigerian led ECOMOG force that had been called in by the Kabbah government.

The Security Council selected General Vijay Jetley of India to serve as the commander of UNAMSIL. More than half of the 11,000 soldiers that were supposed to comprise UNAMSIL were to come from Nigeria with the rest coming from India, Jordan, Guinea, Kenya, and Zambia. The UNAMSIL force consisted of six infantry battalions and a rapid reaction force. The Nigerian contingent, however, operated independent of the UN military commander since it was already on the ground in Sierra Leone as the UNAMSIL was being organized. Paragraph 12 of UN Resolution 1270 contained a vague call for unity of effort, stating that the UN "Stresses the need for close cooperation and coordination between ECOMOG and UNAMSIL in carrying out their respective tasks, and welcomes the intended establishment of joint operations centres at headquarters and, if necessary, also at subordinate levels in the field." This call for cooperation fell far short of unity of command. The presence of a large number of Nigerian troops nominally under UNAMSIL command did not reduce the suspicion among the AFRC and RUF fighters in Sierra Leone that it would function as a neutral force.

UNAMSIL suffered from an inauspicious beginning as it deployed to Sierra Leone. Soldiers from the various member states arrived in Freetown in waves over several months beginning in January 2000.[5] Most of the national contingents did not bring their own logistical support and quickly found that there was insufficient infrastructure and logistics to accommodate them, particularly when they moved out of Freetown into the countryside. As military equipment was shipped into the port of Freetown, it was placed in areas without security. As a result, much of the initial load of military equipment was stolen and either sold on the black market or appropriated by various criminal sources. When they finally received their equipment, they began to deploy throughout the country where 40,000 to 50,000 combatants were operating. Many of the soldiers spoke different languages, which caused issues with command and control.

The security situation was not stable and the DDR process began quite slowly because many armed fighters refused to submit themselves to the process.[6] The first DDR camps were often ill-equipped and resembled prisoner of war compounds in appearance, surrounded by high fences and barbed wire. The presence of Nigerian troops in some of the DDR camps angered RUF and CDF forces. When entering the compound, the combatant turned in his weapon in exchange for food and clothing to begin his six week stay in the DDR camp. The ex-combatants lived in makeshift tents surrounded by dirt courtyards. Former combatants were debriefed and took part in job training—primarily in carpentry and masonry. After completing the DDR process, UN officials issued each former combatant an ID card and $15 in transportation vouchers to go anywhere in the country. Each ex-combatant was expected to obtain his own job. Life in the camps was fraught with unrest and trouble.[7] The UN and the government were unable to meet the inflated expectations of Sierra Leoneans who expected the DDR process to provide instant prosperity and peace. This caused additional frustration among all parties who were already reluctant signatories to the Lome Agreement.

The Lome Agreement guaranteed United Nation officials and UNAMSIL unhindered and safe access to all areas in the country. Unfortunately, as peacekeepers deployed to areas outside of Freetown, they often encountered tense and volatile security situations. The withdrawal of ECOMOG forces and the failure to create effective Sierra Leone police and military units before UNAMSIL arrived proved fatal. In trying to maintain its credibility as a neutral force between the government and rebel forces, General Jetley chose not to grant the authority to use force to compel disarmament or even to defend the UN DDR camps from attack. In spite of the ceasefire agreement, RUF fighters operated freely throughout the country. The peacekeepers were denied freedom of movement and were subjected to ambushes and illegal roadblocks throughout Sierra Leone by armed fighters, mostly RUF factions.[8] After each skirmish, the RUF leader, Foday Sankoh, was contacted about resolving the problem, but usually to no avail. Instead, Sankoh often blamed the government or UNAMSIL for the skirmishes. It was quite obvious that Sankoh was deliberately undermining the Lome Agreement by refusing to order his RUF fighters to undergo the DDR process.

In response to the surprise Nigerian withdrawal from Sierra Leone and the lack of ECOMOG cooperation with the UNAMSIL headquarters, the UN increased the size of UNAMSIL from 6,000 to 11,000 troops under Resolution 1289 which passed on 7 February 2000. This was supposed to include an additional six infantry battalions and more UN observers to offset the withdrawal of Nigerian ECOMOG units in the spring.[9] Expressing its frustration with the deteriorating security situation, paragraph 10 of Resolution 1289 granted UNAMSIL much wider freedom to use military force in the performance of its mission:

> (a) To provide security at key locations and Government buildings, in particular in Freetown, important intersections and major airports, including Lungi airport;
>
> (b) To facilitate the free flow of people, goods and humanitarian
>
> assistance along specified thoroughfares;
>
> (c) To provide security in and at all sites of the disarmament,
>
> demobilization and reintegration programme;
>
> (d) To coordinate with and assist, in common areas of deployment, the Sierra Leone law enforcement authorities in the discharge of their responsibilities;
>
> (e) To guard weapons, ammunition and other military equipment collected from ex-combatants and to assist in their subsequent disposal or destruction, authorizes UNAMSIL to take the necessary action to fulfill the additional tasks set out above, and affirms that, in the discharge of its mandate, UNAMSIL may take the necessary action to ensure the security and freedom of movement of its personnel and, within its capabilities and areas of deployment, to afford protection to civilians under imminent threat of physical violence, taking into account the responsibilities of the Government of Sierra Leone.[10]

Despite this key change in mandate, however, General Jetley refused to change his policy of strict UNAMSIL neutrality and only allowed his units to use force to defend themselves and unarmed civilians if they came under direct attack. Rebel forces grew bolder as the result of UNAMSIL's failure to respond to repeated provocations throughout Sierra Leone. RUF forces even blocked the deployment of Indian and Ghanaian elements from deploying to the eastern Bendu half of the country.[11] A report from the office of Secretary-General of the United Nations described one of many such incidents:

> On 22 April, a group of some 20 RUFP fighters prevented UNAMSIL military observers from entering the premises of the disarmament, demobilization and reintegration reception center of Magburaka (near Makeni). They also alleged that UNAMSIL soldiers, who were providing security at that location, had taken some ammunition belonging to the RUFP. A small-scale scuffle ensued, after which UNAMSIL troops at the site decided to withdraw temporarily to avoid escalation. The Makeni/Magburaka area remained very tense and subsequently became the scene of the first attacks by RUFP on UNAMSIL troops.[12]

Nigeria completed the withdrawal of its troops from Sierra Leone in late April, leaving the country without its largest and most powerful military contingent.[13]

On 4 May 2000, the very day that ECOMOG transferred its responsibilities to UNAMSIL, the RUF attacked and "detained" a contingent of Kenyan UNAMSIL soldiers in the Kono diamond mining region near the town of Makeni, about 70 kilometers east of Freetown. Some 200 Zambian UNAMSIL soldiers who had been sent to relieve the captive Kenyans were also taken hostage along with their armored personnel carriers. The Zambians then surrendered to the RUF on 6 May, bringing the total number of hostages held by the RUF to over 500.

Soon, RUF forces, using the armored personnel carriers and other weapons seized from the UN forces, began to advance towards Freetown. The imminent collapse of the DDR process called for by the Lome Agreement, and the all too obvious shortcomings of UNAMSIL forces led to calls for a new military intervention to save UNAMSIL and the government of Sierra Leone. On 4 May 2000 the UN Secretary-General, Kofi Annan, requested that the United Kingdom and other countries intervene to save the UNAMSIL mission from collapse.

Great Britain to the Rescue: Operation PALLISER

The British government, at the request of the UN and President Kabbah, immediately sent an Operational Liaison and Reconnaissance Team (OLRT) led by Brigadier General David Richards to Freetown on 5 May

2000 to assess the situation. Richards was no stranger to Freetown, having led a team from the HMS *Norfolk* that returned the British High Commissioner to his embassy in January 2000.[14] The team was directed to plan for the possible evacuation of Commonwealth citizens. Richards' OLRT arrived in Freetown early on 6 May and quickly determined that a non-combatant evacuation operation (NEO) could not be conducted without troops to secure the airport and the assembly point and requested troops for that purpose. He would also need airlift from the Freetown assembly point to Lungi airport across the bay because RUF forces blocked the so-called horseshoe road that connected them.[15] It was quite clear that neither UNAMSIL forces nor SLA units were capable of providing security.

British soldiers from the Special Air Service (SAS) and the 1st Battalion of the Parachute Regiment (1 PARA) rapidly deployed to a Forward Mounting Base at Dakar, Senegal on 6 May. They were alerted to this mission just the day before and were able to complete their deployment by the close of the day on 8 May. British forces were able to take advantage of their newly created Joint Force Headquarters at Northwood, UK, a rapidly deployable, joint military headquarters created for exactly this kind of mission. The JFHQ quickly fell in on the OLRT with Brigadier Richards as it commander, collocated with the British High Commissioner.[16] They would be supported by sizeable British naval forces. HMS *Ocean*, a helicopter carrier with Royal Marines led the Amphibious Ready Group then operating in the Mediterranean, about a week away. Four CH-47 Chinook helicopters made the 3,500 mile journey from the UK to Sierra Leone in only 30 hours. The British force, which eventually numbered roughly 5000 troops, operated under a Commonwealth mandate rather than under UN command.[17]

Under the command of Brigadier Richards, Operation PALLISER began with a helicopter assault led by the troops of the SAS and a company of paratroopers of the 1 PARA. The paratroopers quickly secured the Lungi International Airport across the bay from Freetown and established their headquarters there on 7 May. Just as quickly, other UK troops seized the Freetown peninsula and secured the British high commissioner's residence.[18] Once on the ground, the UK commander began meeting with officials from the Sierra Leone government and the United Nations, who were in complete disarray and near collapse as rumors that RUF troops were less than twenty miles from Freetown and preparing to attack. Richards also met with the leaders of various armed factions roaming the streets of Freetown. After assessing the situation Brigadier Richards decided to greatly expand his mission to include saving the UNAMSIL mission from collapse. He quickly dispatched British officers to provide military advice and resolve to UNAMSIL units and Sierra Leone Army units at key points in and around the city, including the key town of Waterloo, twenty kilometers south of Freetown on the horseshoe road. He also discouraged the armed factions from joining the fighting by demonstrating the resolve of the UK and UNAMSIL to remain in control.[19] The British naval force was also anchored close off the Freetown harbor while British aircraft conducted demonstrations overhead, including dropping leaflets discouraging anyone from interfering with British forces.[20]

On 8 May some ten thousand Freetown residents and government soldiers marched on the residence of RUFP leader Sankoh with authorization of the government. They carried placards with inscriptions directed at Sankoh, such as "No Violence Sankoh," "Enough is Enough," and "Sankoh: Our People are dying."[21] Sankoh was informed about the march in advance and had over 150 members of the RUF at his home for protection. UNAMSIL had also placed 30 armed soldiers around the house. UNAMSIL peacekeepers were unable to keep the crowd away from the house and they soon began throwing stones, bottles, and sticks at the house. UNAMSIL personnel fired a warning shot in the air in a misguided attempt to disperse the mob. RUF soldiers in Sankoh's resident opened fire on the crowd and a battle ensued as armed civilians and soldiers in the crowd returned fire. UNAMSIL soldiers retreated from the area. Many RUF members were killed by the mob and the house was looted and ransacked. By the end of the day, over 40 civilians had been killed and several people wounded. During the panic, Sankoh escaped, dressed as a woman, into the forest behind his house.[22]

Because of the deteriorating security situation in Freetown and the 8 May riots, the British High Commissioner in Freetown formally asked Brigadier Richards to begin the NEO. 1 PARA troops immediately secured the Mammy Yoko Hotel and on 9 May 2000, nearly 500 of the 1,000 British citizens were evacuated by four Chinook helicopters to Senegal.[23] The other 600 either chose to remain in Freetown because of the British military presence or lived in outlying areas and considered their safety adequate.[24]

With Lungi International Airport secure and the NEO complete, UNAMSIL and SLA units, with British advice and advisors, began to turn the tide against RUF forces. British leaders assisted SLA and UNAMSIL units with military planning and technical advice and by 15 May, they had driven RUF forces several miles back from outskirts of Freetown. The British government formally expanded the initial NEO mission to include three new tasks (already begun by Brigadier Richards): support to UNAMSIL, support to the SLA, and preparation for humanitarian tasks.[25] Brigadier Richards moved the main headquarters of the JFHQ from Dakar to Freetown to join with his forward command element on the 18th and 19th of May.[26] British firepower and resolve quickly put RUF forces on the defensive and bolstered the flagging morale of UNAMSIL and SLA forces. On 17 May, 1 PARA units identified about 40 RUF moving toward their positions near Lungi Lol, just north of Lungi Airport. The rebels engaged the PARA position and the British responded with full force. As one author later wrote, "the psychological effect of the engagement was immense in deterring the RUF and in further enhancing the reputation of the British troops in the eyes of the UNAMSIL and Sierra Leonean forces."[27]

The UN hastily arranged a summit meeting at Conakry in Guinea and invited the presidents of Liberia, Guinea, Sierra Leone, and a special representative of the UN. The summit was chaired by President Konare of Mali. Participants condemned the RUF attacks and the detention of the UN peacekeepers. They further mandated that Liberian President Charles Taylor become personally involved in the crisis to ensure the release of the detainees and to return the RUF to the peace process.[28] RUF fighters released their UN hostages beginning on 16 May. In response to this crisis, the UN authorized an additional peacekeeping contingent, bringing the total UNAMSIL force to 13,000 with the passage of UN Resolution 1299 on 19 May 2000.[29]

On 17 May 2000, Foday Sankoh and his bodyguard came out of hiding and into public view. As he was walking around near his house, Sankoh was recognized by local residents who alerted a militia commander known as Black Scorpion.[30] Black Scorpion laid an impromptu ambush, killing Sankoh's bodyguards and wounding Sankoh.[31] Prior to being turned over to British soldiers, he was stripped and forced to walk through the streets naked. The humiliated warlord was charged with the murder of the demonstrators in a Freetown municipal court and placed in prison awaiting trial.[32]

The Amphibious Ready Group (ARG) that had departed from Marseilles, France, arrived off the coast of Sierra Leone on May 12th and 13th. The ARG included the HMS *Ocean*, the Royal Fleet Auxiliary ships *Fort George* and *Fort Austin,* and logistics ships *Sir Tristram* and *Sir Bedevere*, as well as the frigate HMS *Chatham*. In addition, the aircraft carrier *Illustrious* and its 13 Harrier jet aircraft had departed Lisbon, Portugal and joined the ARG off Sierra Leone. The 42 Commando Royal Marines from the ARG took over the mission and relieved the troops of the 1 PARA on 30 May. Their mission—still under Richards—was to secure the release of the hostages, and strengthen the UNAMSIL and government forces.[33]

With the hostages released, Brigadier Richards turned his attention to training UNAMSIL and SLA soldiers. Once the planning cell was established, Richards provided key liaison officers, gave technical advice on a range of issues, and basically began directing the SLA/UNAMSIL campaign plan.[34] According to Richards, "the most decisive factors were persuading them, at least temporarily, to move from a peacekeeping to a conventional defensive posture, and convincing them that the RUF were not supermen."[35] Now with a formidable Royal Navy presence off the coast of Freetown, the British were able to quickly sling-load heavy artillery and ammunition to the forces in Sierra Leone. Liaison officers were exchanged and key meetings were established between SLA and the British on a daily basis.[36] By the end of May 2000, UNAMSIL, SLA, and British forces, with the help of a Jordanian Special Forces battalion drove the RUF forces far away from Freetown and the Lungi airport. The tide had turned in favor of the government and the UN.

British forces departed Sierra Leone on 15 June and Operation PALLISER came to an end. With renewed confidence UNAMSIL and SLA soldiers were able to take over positions previously secured by British soldiers and began actively fighting and winning battles with the RUF. As the British main body departed Freetown they left a training contingent of about 200 British soldiers stationed at Camp Waterloo, about 20-km southeast of Freetown, and who were responsible for training SLA soldiers in infantry skills.[37] With RUF leader Sankoh in a Freetown prison, General Issa Sesay took over control of the RUF Party and RUF military forces, with Sankoh's approval. Sesay began to work with UNAMSIL and began to actively work for a peace settlement between the RUFP and the government. Despite being Sankoh's deputy, the change in leadership and policy caused a split in the RUFP and many deserted its ranks.[38]

Unfortunately, fighting continued between UNAMSIL and rebel groups in outlying areas around Freetown. One such rebel group, known as the West Side Boys (WSB), nearly erased the gains made by the British and the UN.

West Side Boys

The WSB gang included former members of the SLA, former members of the RUFP, criminals from Pademba Road Prison released during the 1997 coup, and ordinary civilians who were recruited by the rebel gang members. Many of the rebels were captured children under the age of 15 who were indoctrinated into the group and forced to commit atrocities on ordinary citizens. Some of the children were abducted after watching their parents die at the hands of the recruiters while others were forced to torture their parents to death.[39]

The group was known for wearing bizarre clothing to include women's wigs and flip-flops and being almost perpetually drunk with homemade palm wine. The WSB were heavy users of locally grown marijuana and heroin bought with alluvial diamonds. Diamonds were also used to purchase many of their weapons, including ZPU-2 antiaircraft guns, RPG-7 grenade launchers, 81-mm mortars, AK-47 rifles, and SLR rifles. Most of their vehicles had been hijacked from UN food convoys or captured from the SLA. The WSB operated in and around Freetown, and in the northeastern parts of Sierra Leone, often setting up road-blocks to extort money and goods from travelers. During the day, those who encountered the group paid them off with alcohol, drugs, tobacco, or equipment carried in the vehicle. During the evening, when the WSB were high on alcohol or drugs, travelers were often fired upon and killed.[40]

Great Britain Returns: Vignette on Operation BARRAS

On Friday, 25 August 2000, British Major Alan Marshall, stationed at Benguema Training Camp decided to make a visit to one of UNAMSIL's battalions near the town of Masiaka, about 65-kilometers east of Freetown. Marshall and his men were part of the stay-behind British training contingent. Accompanying him on this visit was an SLA liaison officer and 11 soldiers from the Royal Irish Regiment. After visiting with Colonel Jehad al-Widyan, commander of the UNAMSIL battalion, he decided to take his patrol to the WSB base in nearby Magbeni. Marshall received an intelligence report that only a few rebels were present at the base and he wanted to check out the situation.[41] His three Land Rovers were armed with .50-caliber heavy machine guns and the soldiers with SA80 rifles. As the patrol approached Magbeni, located 50 miles east of the capital in Freetown, the WSB blocked the road and denied them movement. Major Marshall tried to reason with them, but they insisted that he wait until their leader, 24-year old "Brigadier" Foday Kallay arrived.[42]

As they waited, Major Marshall carried on a conversation with the boys and offered them cigarettes. Communication with the base at Benguema Training Camp was established via radio and the base camp was informed that the patrol was being detained. Once Kallay arrived, the situation turned tense. Kallay began issuing orders to his armed soldiers, became angry with Marshall for entering an unauthorized area without coordination, and surrounded the patrol with soldiers and a captured SLA truck mounted with a 14.5-mm heavy machine gun. As Marshall made attempts to reason with the WSB, he was physically beaten. Within 5 minutes, the rest of the Royal Irish soldiers were overwhelmed, disarmed, stripped, and taken by canoes upstream, across Rokel River, to Gberi Bana, Kallay's headquarters.[43]

Communication between the WSB leader Kallay and the British base was established using the patrol's radio. Lieutenant Colonel Simon Fordham of the Royal Irish Regiment led a team of negotiators from the Ministry of Defense, Freetown Police, United Nation personnel, a Special Air Service (SAS) assessment team, and Major Johnny Paul Koroma, the former coup leader and now a member of the Sierra Leonean Government. A face-to-face meeting was held on 27 August and the WSB demanded the release of Foday Sankoh, the RUFP leader, along with food, medicine, a generator, and a satellite phone in exchange for the detained soldiers. The team met all of the WSB demands except for the release of Foday Sankoh, and the WSB released 5 of the 11 soldiers on 30 August 2000. The WSB continued to hold six soldiers and the SLA liaison officer.[44] The WSB stressed that the other demands needed to be met for the release of the remaining soldiers.

Negotiations continued with the WSB on 31 August but the situation, described by the team on the ground, was becoming delicate and volatile.[45] Kallay used the satellite phone to demand the current government of Sierra Leone step down. Unbeknownst to Kallay, the negotiators gave him the phone to get a precise location via signal interception on where the remaining hostages were located. As the team made further contact with the WSB, negotiations failed. Kallay threatened to kill the hostages if his demands were not met. Prime Minister Tony Blair directed the British Chief of Defense Staff, General Sir Charles Guthrie, to devise a rescue plan.

As the planning mission began, the British established several observation posts composed of four man teams of SAS soldiers inserted from Rokel River by the Special Boat Service (SBS) to pinpoint locations near Magbeni and Gberi Bana.[46] The SAS soldiers were augmented by a number of SBS soldiers who had been clandestinely flown into the country to prepare for a possible hostage rescue mission. The team was to provide intelligence information to include movements around the WSB base camp, possible helicopter landing sites, weapons, location of hostages, and vehicles. The intelligence information was conveyed to the higher headquarters planning cell via the patrol's radio operator using a satellite link.[47]

Intelligence reports from the observation points told of the erratic behavior of Kallay, mock executions, positions of heavy weapons, and the location of the captured vehicles. It was reported that the seven hostages were being held at a village named Gberi Bana about 400 meters away from the rebels at Magbeni and across Rokel River.

In addition, the SAS teams reported that the WSB soldier strength on Gberi Bana and Magbeni was between 50 and 100 in each camp.[48] The WSB gang members were armed with AK-47 rifles, rocket propelled grenade launchers, 60-mm, 81-mm and 120-mm mortars and Fabric National (FN) sniper rifles.[49] In addition to these weapons, surveillance indicated that the WSB had pick-up trucks with mounted machine guns, the Bedford 4-ton captured from the SLA, and the three Land Rovers. In terms of position, the mortars and machine guns in Magbeni secured the approaches from the south, and were able to engage targets across the Rokel River at Gberi Bana.

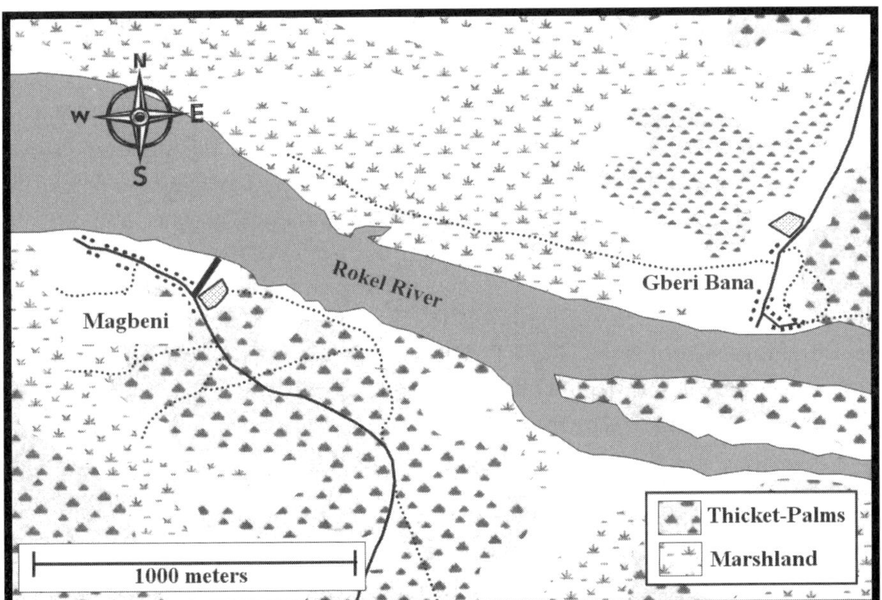

Map 6. Operation BARRAS area of operations.

Magbeni and Gberi Bana were surrounded by dense jungle vegetation, mangrove swamps, murky marshland, and low palm woodlands. At Gberi Bana, due to the defensive positioning of weapons from Magbeni to the south and swamps and dense vegetation on the east and west, the only area that needed to be secured was to the north. Only one road went into Gberi Bana and that road was heavily guarded. Gberi Bana made an excellent prison with very little possibility of escape by foot. Gberi Bana itself consisted of five low mud and cement buildings. Magbeni consisted of a roadway along the Rokel River with 29 war-torn buildings and large areas of jungle vegetation that could provide cover for both defensive and offensive operations.

The UK Ministry of Defense alerted the 1st Battalion, 1 Parachute Regiment on 30 August 2000 for a possible rescue mission. Major Matthew Lowe was selected as the task force commander due to his experience in jungle operations. In addition, many of his non-commissioned officers had just returned from Operation PALLISER and were familiar with the situation.[50] Other forces were also alerted for possible deployment, including the Royal Fleet Auxiliary (RFA) *Argus* and elements of the Royal Air Force (RAF). As a contingency plan, two Lynx helicopters were taken by C-130 Hercules transport aircraft to Dakar in Senegal and then on to Lungi airport near Freetown. The two Lynxes and the three RAF Chinooks already in the country were then deployed to a small airfield at Hastings, about 25 miles south of Freetown. As the planning continued, the soldiers of the parachute regiment began their field training exercise in England.

The British JFHQ in Freetown devised a plan to have the 1 PARA to attack the Magbeni camp and the SAS troops to attack Gberi Bana where the soldiers were being held hostage. On 3 September the 1 PARA deployed their planners to Dakar, the capital of Senegal, approximately 500 miles from Freetown, to begin planning their part of rescue mission. The team was supplied with maps, aerial photography, intelligence updates, as well as intelligence information from the local government regarding the surroundings of both Gberi Bana and Magbeni.[51] As the planning cell continued its operation in Dakar, a similar planning cell began work in Freetown at the British military headquarters. This SAS-led team concentrated on the extraction of hostages. On 6 September, the PARA task force, approximately 150 soldiers, deployed to Dakar for live-fire exercises, familiarization training, and acclimatization.

The British Ministry of Defense asked journalists in Britain not to speculate about the possible deployment. A news story written in the

Sierra Leone Press, located in Freetown, about the deployment of the PARA to Senegal actually provided some cover for the SAS's operations in and around the objective.[52] As the crisis continued, a medical team was positioned in a freight container on the Royal Fleet Auxiliary (RFA) *Sir Percivale* to conduct possible triage and medical support operations. Alongside the *Percivale* was the *Argyll*, a warship complete with landing decks for aircraft. Both ships were anchored off the shores of Freetown.[53]

On 9 September, Kallay insisted that he would not release the hostages until a new interim government was established. After 14 days of negotiation, there appeared to be little hope of securing the release of the hostages through continued dialogue. British Prime Minister Tony Blair gave the order to launch the rescue mission. The JFHQ was also given permission from President Kabbah to conduct an operation against the WSB at a time of their choosing.[54] All soldiers were moved to Hastings Battle Camp for final coordination. Hastings was only about 15 minutes by air from the objective.

H-hour for Operation BARRAS was set for 0616 hours on 10 September. The early morning landing gave an element of surprise and assurance that the WSB were at their weakest. Speed and surprise was essential if the captives were to be seized before their WSB captors could kill them. At H-hour two RAF Lynx and three Chinook helicopters departed Hastings for the short flight to the WSB camp. The Lynx helicopters, equipped with night vision equipment, heavy machine guns, and thermal night imagers, provided overhead security for the Chinooks carrying PARA and SAS soldiers. The attack helicopters approached at a very low level along the river to ensure maximum surprise. Once near the target, the two Lynx split with one attacking from the south and the other from the north.[55] Although UNAMSIL units were not informed about the operation, they were given the mission to secure and block positions on the road to Magbeni.[56]

UK planners designed Operation BARRAS as a simultaneous, two-pronged attack. Two platoons of 1 PARA troopers air assaulted from two helicopters and landed in the jungle area south of Magbeni.

Their mission was to neutralize weapons covering Gberi Bana to the north, defeat the forces on the ground, secure a landing zone east of the town, and recover the Land Rovers. The PARA landed in marshy water and moved 150 meters to the tree line.[57] As a heavy machine gun fired at the Chinooks from Magbeni, the Lynx helicopter was able to identify the location and raked it with its 12.7-mm machine gun, knocking out the

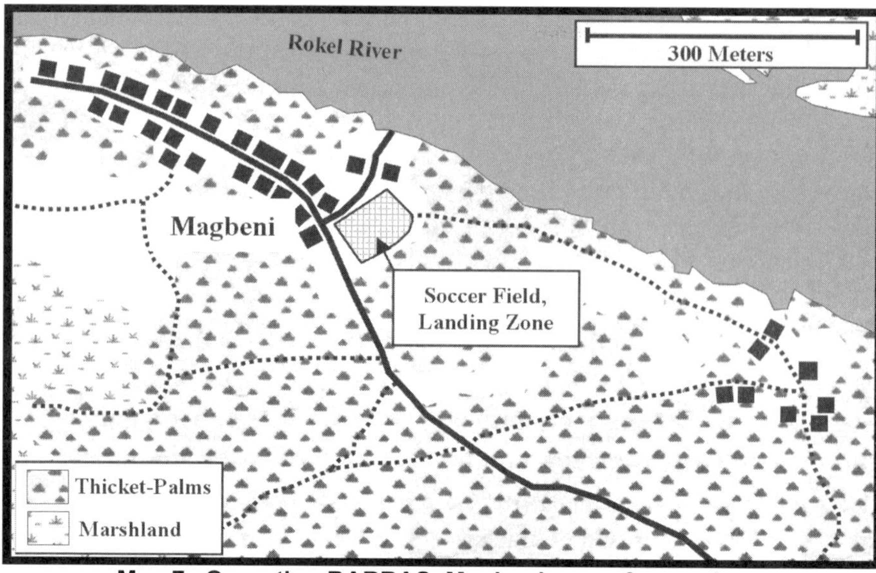

Map 7. Operation BARRAS–Magbeni area of operations.

heavy machine gun and its gunners. The PARAs moved from the tree-line to the huts in a west-to-east sweep in three platoon-level attacks and quickly accomplished their objective.

Frogmen of the SBS launched the second prong of the attack by crossing Rokel River underwater and opening fire as they emerged in the darkness. At the same time SAS snipers came from their hiding places in the swamps near Gberi Bana and surprised the WSB with a barrage of fire and flash-bang grenades.

As the WSB adjusted to the barrage of fire, they responded with their own fire. A Chinook helicopter carrying the SAS rescue force was the target. While unloading a platoon of SAS soldiers, Brad Tinnion exited the Chinook and was shot by an insurgent. WSB fighters fired RPGs at the Chinook in an effort to destroy it, but both rounds missed. The SAS troops made their approach to the huts nearby where the hostages were held, killed the WSB members guarding the hut, and escorted the hostages and wounded onto the Chinook helicopter. As they swept through the area, they also captured Kallay, who was hiding under bedding in one of the WSB huts.[58]

British forces accomplished the rescue mission, from landing in Gberi Bana and loading hostages onto the Chinook, in only 20 minutes. At the

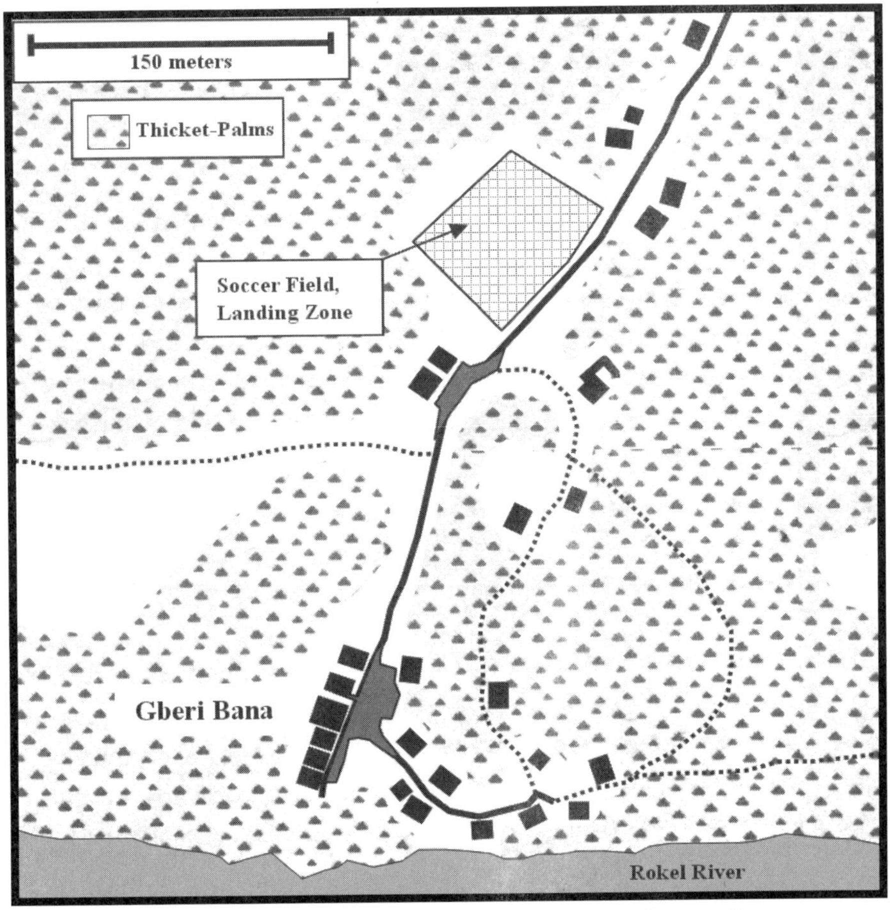

Map 8. Operation BARRAS–Gberi Bana area of operations.

nearby Magbeni WSB camp, fighting continued and the PARA remained in the area until 1600, scouring the jungle looking for WSB fighters that fled the initial assault and recovering the three captured Land Rovers and other weapons. British forces killed 25 and captured 18 WSB members. Three of the WSB casualties were women, one of which was the notorious Mammy Kallay, wife of Foday Kallay, who was a particularly ruthless supporter of her husband.[59] As the Chinook returned to the RFA *Sir Percivale*, anchored in Freetown, SAS soldier Brad Tinnon died. Twelve other soldiers were wounded, but none critically. In addition to the British hostages, the rescuers freed 22 Sierra Leoneans captives from Gberi Bana: 17 men used for forced labor and 5 women abducted for sex.[60] Operation BARRAS, a brief subset of Operation PALLISER, ended at 1600 when the remaining SAS and PARA withdrew.

Continuing Progress

Progress made by UNAMSIL and the Sierra Leone government after the British intervention in May 2000 began to stall by October in face of continued resistance by RUF forces, particularly in the far eastern and southern parts of the country. The brief capture of British soldiers by the West Side Boys in September contributed to the sense the combined UNAMSIL and SLA offensive had lost momentum. RUF forces continued to receive support from Charles Taylor in Liberia and were beginning to operate inside the borders of Guinea, plus they continued to control the diamond producing regions of southern Sierra Leone.[61] The UN also changed commanders for UNAMSIL during the fall of 2000. Indian General Jetley departed Sierra Leone in September after having been stricken by malaria. His deputy, Nigerian General Garbe took command. The presence of a Nigerian officer in command of UNAMSIL appears to have angered the RUF because of Nigeria's long history of supporting sides in Sierra Leone's civil war. Indian forces, as well as those from Jordan, withdrew from UNAMSIL because of the shift of UNAMSIL from strict neutrality to enforcement of UN Resolution 1270.[62]

In the face of increased RUF resistance and the stalling of UNAMSIL operations, the British government announced to the world that it was prepared to return to Sierra Leone to restore UNAMSIL effectiveness. Thus, in October 2000 the UK launched Operation SILKMAN, deploying Brigadier Richards and the Joint Force HQ back to Freetown and dispatching the ARG to the shores of Sierra Leone. The six ships of the ARG conducted exercises, and helicopter overflights along the coast. The Marines of 42 Commando even marched through the city of Freetown in a show of force. Brigadier Richards and the JFHQ provided military planning advice, technical support, and another dose of resolve to UNAMSIL and the SLA. Then on 1 November 2001 General Garba was replaced by Lieutenant General Daniel Opande of Kenya as the new UNAMSIL Commander. British Brigadier Alastair Duncan was appointed UNAMSIL's Chief of Staff. At the same time, Guinean forces imposed a major defeat on RUF forces operating in that country and international pressure on Charles Taylor finally ended Liberia's open support for the RUF. The RUF found itself on the defensive everywhere, its original backers in Liberia withdrawing their support, and its enemies were growing in strength and resolve. After only a month of renewed UNAMSIL and SLA attacks, the RUF leader, Issay Sesay, signed another cease-fire agreement at Abidjan, Ivory Coast on 10 November.[63] Sesay later admitted the British intervention in Sierra Leone and the resulting improvements in the UNAMSIL and the SLA forced him to seek peace. As Brigadier Richards phrased it, "They had succumbed to the British aim of 'persuading the RUF of the inevitability of defeat.'"[64] Operation SILKMAN came to an end and Brigadier Richards departed Sierra Leone for the last time in mid-November, after only six weeks.

Epilogue

In 2001 and 2002 the UNAMSIL mission grew in strength and reached 17,500 troops, the largest peacekeeping mission in the world at that time and became increasingly effective. The UN finally targeted the illicit diamond trade which was the financial source of so much of the fighting in Sierra Leone. The UN Security Council adopted Resolution 1343, sponsored by the United States, on 7 March 2001. This resolution demanded that the Government of Liberia expel all RUF members, end financial and military support to the RUF, cease direct or indirect import of rough diamonds, and ground all Liberia-registered aircraft until registration and ownership could be updated. The Resolution also demanded that other countries refuse to allow so called "conflict diamonds" to enter into the world market.[65] The US then led the effort to impose a full scale embargo on diamond trading with Liberia. Coupled with renewed UNAMSIL pressure on remaining RUF forces, these measures broke the back of RUF resistance.[66]

The illegal trade in diamonds that financed much of the ten year civil war in Sierra Leone for a brief time attracted the attention of al-Qaeda terrorists during the UNAMSIL mission. As it had done elsewhere, the terrorist group saw the opportunity to finance its operations in the chaotic regions of Sierra Leone that were not controlled by the government. Douglas Farrah, the bureau chief for the *Washington Post* in West Africa, broke the story on 1 November 2001, relying on information provided to him by a journalist named Cindor Reeves who was the younger brother of Charles Taylor's first wife.[67] Reeves identified three of the faces in a magazine story as people he met while at the Kono mine, near Kailahun—all three were connected to Osama bin Laden's al-Qaeda terrorist network. The exposure of the al-Qaeda network led to its dissolution.

The DDR process rapidly became more effective in mid 2001 after the diamond embargoes took effect and after UNAMSIL began to more aggressively challenge RUF holdouts. When the UN declared the Disarmament process complete on 17 January 2002, UN officials had collected over 45,000 weapons while over 70,000 fighters completed this part of the DDR process, double the number that had been expected.[68] The reintegration phase of the DDR process continued into 2003 but continued to be hampered by a lack of funds and job opportunities in the private economy. In January 2002 the Kabbah government of Sierra Leone and the UN reached agreement to stand up both a Truth and Reconciliation Commission and a Special Court to facilitate the reintegration process, the restoration of civil society, and to bring justice to those guilty of the worst crimes during the previous decade of civil war.

In March 2003 the Court indicted AFRC/RUF leaders Foday Sankoh, Johnny Koroma, Sam Bockarie, Issa Sesay, and many others for war crimes. Bockarie and Koroma were then in Liberia fighting with Charles Taylor. Bockarie was killed and Johnny Koroma has disappeared. Former Liberian President Charles Taylor who had provided much of the RUF's support was indicted in July 2003 but was offered asylum in Nigeria by President Obasanjo.[69]

Sierra Leone and the UN conducted presidential and parliamentary elections in May 2002 and President Kabbah was re-elected to power with over 70% of the vote in what was determined to be a free and fair election. During his address at the opening of the new parliamentary assembly, President Kabbah spoke the following words:

> All Sierra Leoneans, at home and abroad, suffered considerable loss. Some lost their cherished and loved ones, others their belongings, and still others, their dignity and honor. The bitter experience of armed conflict will linger in our memories for as long as we need to remind ourselves of the mistakes that we should never ever make again.[70]

The civil war in Sierra Leone was officially declared over in January 2003. Former RUF leader Foday Sankoh died peacefully in UN custody in a Freetown hospital on 30 July 2003 while awaiting trial by the UN Sierra Leone Special Court, thus escaping justice for his crimes.[71] After a new Liberian government was elected in early 2006, the Nigerian government announced on 25 March 2006 that it would turn Taylor over to Liberia to face charges in Liberian courts. Taylor managed to slip away from his residence in Calabar, Nigeria the following day, but was caught on 29 March attempting to flee to the nation of Cameroon. Nigerian authorities handed him over to the UN in Sierra Leone. The Sierra Leone Special Court requested permission to use the facilities of the International Criminal Court in The Hague for Taylor's trial. His trial began in June 2007 and as of March 2008 it is still underway.[72]

Summary: Analysis of the UNAMSIL and UK Missions

The UNAMSIL mission to Sierra Leone suffered from a variety of problems in early 2000 which led to the need for UK intervention to rescue it. The polyglot nature of UNAMSIL's military forces presented a host of problems. UNAMSIL was plagued by inadequate logistics, equipment, and intelligence. The UN DDR mission was also hampered by a lack of resources, further weakening UNAMSIL's credibility. The chief shortcoming, however, was the mismatch between UNAMSIL's expansive mission to enforce security, support the government, and assist the UN DDR process, and the still violent situation in Sierra Leone.

UNAMSIL forces deployed to Sierra Leone with inadequate logistics capabilities. This lack of capability contributed to the long delay between the signing of the Lome Agreement in July 1999, the UN Security Council authorization of the mission in late October 1999, and the actual arrival of UNAMSIL forces in January 2000. Even after these delays, upon their arrival in Freetown UN forces lacked basic infrastructure and self-sustainment to include tents, vehicles, and communications equipment. Gangs, criminals, and others even managed to steal much of the first shipments of UN equipment when it eventually arrived in Freetown. These shortages and shortcomings further delayed the start of their DDR observer mission for several weeks and gave the RUF yet more time to rethink their peace agreement.

In the fall of 1999 as the UN resolutions authorizing UNAMSIL were being negotiated, the Nigerian government argued in the UN that its military should provide the commander for UNAMSIL forces since they had prior experience and knowledge of Sierra Leone. The United Nations, however, insisted that Indian General Jetley serve as the commander of all UNAMSIL forces in order to demonstrate the UN's impartiality during the DDR process. Nigeria then decided to withdraw its troops in early 2000 leaving Sierra Leone with no military force to provide security. The UNAMSIL headquarters and its newly arriving troops had to set up operations before they could take effective control of the Nigerian ECOMOG forces already in Sierra Leone. That never took place because of the vague wording of UN Resolution 1270 regarding ECOMOG's relationship to UNAMSIL. Nigerian troops operated alongside UN troops, but not under any coherent command and control structure.

UNAMSIL intelligence failings were partially responsible for the attack of the RUF leader's home in Freetown that ended UNAMSIL's ability to operate until rescued by British forces later in the year. UN personnel did not have a plan for crowd control at Sankoh's house prior to the public demonstration, although they were warned about the number of people participating in the demonstration. UNAMSIL officials underrated the gravity of the situation and allowed the crowd to surge out of control. Although Sankoh was blamed for the murder of the civilians, an equal amount of responsibility for the disaster could be placed at the feet of UNAMSIL.

UNAMSIL's most significant shortcoming was the disconnect between the chaotic and violent situation inside Sierra Leone and its broad peacekeeping mission. UNAMSIL operated under Chapter VII of the United Nations, which could have authorized it to use force to accomplish its missions. But UN Resolution 1270 envisioned UNAMSIL as a neutral force to an agreement between parties already reconciled to peace, and therefore it limited the use of force to self defense and the protection of civilians under imminent attack. In contrast, the earlier Nigerian led ECOMOG interventions operated in support of the Sierra Leone government against the interests of the RUF and other factions. The UNAMSIL commander, General Jetley, therefore believed that his units must remain neutral and refrain from using force to avoid giving the appearance of favoring one party over another.

But given the violent nature of Sierra Leonean politics and the presence of hundreds of armed groups only nominally under the control of any central leaders, the mission was in fact peace enforcement, not mere peacekeeping. Though an agreement had been signed at Lome, armed factions inside Sierra Leone needed to be persuaded to comply with its mandates. Even after the passage of UN Resolution 1289 in February 2000 granted UNAMSIL wider latitude to enforce the provisions of the Lome Agreement, General Jetley refused to change his rules of engagement. The failure of UNAMSIL units to use military force against non-cooperating armed groups between February and April 2000 undermined their credibility in the eyes of all parties. The embarrassing capture of 500 of its peacekeepers in April 2000 by RUF fighters in Kono essentially brought the mission to a standstill.

Only the intervention of British troops as part of Operation PALLISER in May 2000 managed to set UNAMSIL on the path to success. British military power essentially gave UNAMSIL a shot in the arm when it quickly defeated the armed factions around Freetown that had intimidated UNAMSIL forces. The British forces initially arrived under a Commonwealth mandate to rescue non-combatants. The British Commander, Brigadier David Richards, however, quickly expanded the British role. He has come under some criticism for "driving" the British mission from the scene by his independent actions. Though it is hard to argue with success, and Operation PALLISER was stunningly successful.

The obvious professionalism, audacious leadership, and overwhelming military power of British soldiers intimidated the RUF and others while inspiring UNAMSIL and the government of Sierra Leone. Operation PALLISER was also conducted with great speed. Troops were notified on one day and deployed to a holding area in Senegal the next. They were in Sierra Leone in less than 36 hours and at maximum battle group strength within 64 hours. The remarkable speed at which the British conducted operations also contrasted very favorably with the delays and dithering of UNAMSIL and forced all factions and forces in Sierra Leone to fall into line with UK objectives.

Even the stunning success of Operation PALLISER, however, was tarnished by the embarrassing capture of some of its soldiers by the West Side Boys in September 2000. Major Alan Marshall and the soldiers of his patrol were caught unprepared by the child soldiers of the West Side Boys. Four months of successful operations in Sierra Leone seems to have given the British patrol a false sense of confidence and security that their mere presence and reputation would deter would be opponents. The British troops seemed to have forgotten or underestimated the long standing use of children as soldiers, in Sierra Leone's civil wars. After negotiations failed, British leaders and soldiers executed a nearly perfect raid and hostage rescue in Operation BARRAS. The West Side Boys simply weren't prepared for, or capable of, resisting the overwhelming fire power and skill of the British soldiers of 1 PARA and the SAS. Operation BARRAS should not, however, have been needed. After the British intervention in Sierra Leone in May 2000, both UNAMSIL and the government of Sierra Leone managed to become more effective in implementing the tenets of the 1999 Lome Agreement. It took further military action by the UK and more aggressive UNAMSIL military measures in the fall of 2000, as well as an international diamond embargo against neighboring Liberia, to finally force RUF leader Issay Sessy to capitulate.

Notes

1. United Nations Security Council Resolution 1270 (1999), 22 October 1999, United Nations Security Council, http://www.un.org/Docs/scres/1999/sc99.htm (accessed 18 August 2007).

2. Ibid.

3. Ibid. See also Mirna Galic, "Into the Breach: An Analysis of the United Nations Mission in Sierra Leone," *Stanford Journal of International Relations*, http://www.stanford.edu/group/sjir/3.1.04_galic.html (accessed 18 August 2007).

4. Kofi Annan, "Eighth Report of the Secretary-General on the United Nations Observer Mission in Sierra Leone," *Reports Of The Secretary-General To The Security Council In 1999*, para. 36, http://www.un.org/Docs/sc/reports/1999/sgrep99.htm (accessed 18 August 2007).

5. Galic, "Into the Breach: An Analysis of the United Nations Mission in Sierra Leone."

6. Shalini Chawla, "United Nations Mission in Sierra Leone: A Search for Peace," *Strategic Analysis: A Monthly Journal of the IDSA*, Vol. XXIV No. 9 (December 2000), http://www.ciaonet.org/olj/sa/sa_dec00chs01.html (accessed 10 August 2007).

7. Mark Malan, Phenyo Rakate, and Angela McIntyre, "Peacekeeping in Sierra Leone: UNAMSIL Hits the Home Straight– Chapter 7: Disarmament, Demobilization, and Reintegration," *Institute for Security Studies Monograph Series*, no. 68, http://www.iss.co.za/Pubs/Monographs/No68/Chap7.html (accessed 7 August 2007).

8. United Nations Security Council, *Third report of the Secretary-General on the United Nations mission in Sierra Leone, S/2000/186*, 7 March 2000, paragraph 10, http://www.un.org/Docs/sc/reports/2000/sgrep00.htm (accessed 10 August 2007).

9. United Nations Security Council Resolution 1289 (2000), 7 February 2000, United Nations Security Council, http://www.un.org/Docs/scres/2000/sc2000.htm (accessed 18 August 2007).

10. Ibid.

11. General Sir David Richards, "Sierra Leone–'Pregnant with Lessons?'" in *Royal United Services Institute Whitehall Paper 63–Global Challenges and Africa: Bridging Divides, Dealing with Perceptions, Rebuilding Societies* (August 2004), 9-21.

12. United Nations Security Council, *Fourth Report of the Secretary-General on the United Nations Mission in Sierra Leone, S/2000/455*, 19 May 2000, paragraph 17, http://www.un.org/Docs/sc/reports/2000/sgrep00.htm (accessed 10 August 2007).

13. William J. Lahneman, *Military Intervention: Cases in Context for the Twenty-First Century*, (Oxford: Rowman & Littlefield Publishers, Inc, 2004), 143-145.

14. The UK based mercenary firm, Sandline, was also rumored to have supported the ECOMOG forces that restored President Kabbah to power in the spring of 1999. See the unpublished manuscript by Gwyn Prins, "Strategic Raiding," Combat Studies Institute, Fort Leavenworth, KS.

15. Prins, "Strategic Raiding."

16. Major General David Richards, "Expeditionary Operations: Sierra Leone–Lessons For the Future," *Royal United Services Institute–World Defence Systems*, Issue Four, http://www.sovereign-publications.com/wds-4-articles.htm (accessed 10 August 2007).

17. David Leatherwood, *The Hazards of Strange Bedfellows: The United States, Nigeria, and Peacekeeping in West Africa* (Washington DC: National War College, 2000), http://www.ndu.edu/library/n2/n01LeatherwoodHazards.doc (accessed 3 August 2007).

18. William Fowler, *Operation Barras: The SAS Rescue Mission: Sierra Leone 2000*, (London: Orion Publishing, 2004), 84.

19. Richards, "Expeditionary Operations: Sierra Leone–Lessons For the Future."

20. Andrew Dorman, "The British Experience of Low Intensity Conflict in Sierra Leone," *Defense and Security Analysis Journal*, Volume 23, Number 2 (June 2007), pp. 185-200, http://www.ingentaconnect.com/content/routledg/cdan/2007/00000023/00000002 (accessed 8 August 2007).

21. Truth and Reconciliation Commission of Sierra Leone, *Final Report of the Truth and Reconciliation Commission of Sierra Leone*, Chapter 3, para 1336, 1337, http://trcsierraleone.org/drwebsite/publish/v3a-c1.shtml, (accessed 10 June 2007).

22. Ibid., sections 1406-1422.

23. Richards, "Expeditionary Operations: Sierra Leone–Lessons For the Future."

24. Dorman, "The British Experience of Low Intensity Conflict in Sierra Leone."

25. Richards, "Expeditionary Operations: Sierra Leone–Lessons For the Future."

26. Prins, "Strategic Raiding."

27. Gwyn Prins, *The Heart of War: On Power, Conflict and Obligation in the Twenty-First Century*, (New York: Routledge Publishing, 2002), 203.

28. United Nations Security Council, *Fourth Report of the Secretary-General on the United Nations Mission in Sierra Leone*, para 76.

29. United Nations Security Council Resolution 1299 (2000), 19 May 2000, United Nations Security Council, http://www.un.org/Docs/scres/2000/sc2000.htm (accessed 18 August 2007).

30. Truth and Reconciliation Commission of Sierra Leone, *Final Report of the Truth and Reconciliation Commission of Sierra Leone*, para 1466.

31. Ibid.

32. Lansana Gberie, *A Dirty War in West Africa: The RUF And the Destruction of Sierra Leone*, (Bloomington, IN: Indiana University Press, 2005), 167. The trial was suspended after Sankoh was charged by the UN mandated Special Court for crimes against humanity.

33. Prins, *The Heart of War: On Power, Conflict and Obligation in the Twenty-First Century*.

34. Richards, "Expeditionary Operations: Sierra Leone–Lessons For the Future."

35. Ibid.

36. Ibid.

37. Prins, "Strategic Raiding."

38. Truth and Reconciliation Commission of Sierra Leone, *Final Report of the Truth and Reconciliation Commission of Sierra Leone*, para 1502.

39. David Keen, *Conflict and Collusion in Sierra Leone*, (New York: Palgrave Publishers, 2005), 232-235.

40. BBC, "Sierra Leone Timeline–31 August 2000," BBC News Web site, http://news.bbc.co.uk/2/hi/africa/741070.stm (accessed 10 August 2007).

41. BBC, "UK Captives 'Did Not Liaise with UN'–30 August 2000," BBC News Web site, http://news.bbc.co.uk/2/hi/africa/902266.stm (accessed 10 August 2007). The deputy commander of the UN peacekeeping force in Sierra Leone, Nigeria's General Mohammed Garba, challenged Major Marshall's decision to travel in a dangerous rebel area. According to General Garba, the British soldiers decided to check out the area without coordinating this with the UN. It was later determined that Major Marshall coordinated with Brigadier Gordon Hughes, Commander British Forces in Sierra Leone.

42. Gberie, *A Dirty War in West Africa: The RUF And the Destruction of Sierra Leone*, 174. The rank of Foday Kallay is anywhere from Major to Brigadier General. He is one of the soldiers who plotted and carried out the AFRC coup with Johnny Paul Koroma.

43. Fowler, *Operation Barras: The SAS Rescue Mission: Sierra Leone 2000*, 9-11.

44. BBC, "Sierra Leone hostage talks 'going well'–4 September 2000," BBC News Web site, http://news.bbc.co.uk/2/hi/africa/909045.stm (accessed 10 August 2007).

45. Fowler, *Operation Barras: The SAS Rescue Mission: Sierra Leone 2000*, 114.

46. The exact number of soldiers inserted is not known. The SAS does not disclose information on operations due to their secretive mission. In fact, when the Ministry of Defense released a censored version of Operation BARRAS to the Sierra Leone Press, dated 10 September 2000, no reference is made to the role of the Special Forces unit. It is estimated that as many as 100 SAS were involved in this mission, from planning to completion.

47. Fowler, *Operation Barras: The SAS Rescue Mission: Sierra Leone 2000*, 124 -125.

48. Ibid., 126.

49. Ibid., 126.
50. Ibid., 114.
51. Ibid., 121.
52. Ibid., 122-123.
53. "Argyll Saves 58 From Drowning" *Navy News–Online*, http://www.navynews.co.uk/articles/2000/0008/0000082501.asp (accessed 15 August 2007).
54. Fowler, *Operation Barras: The SAS Rescue Mission: Sierra Leone 2000*, 136.
55. Tom Cooper and Court Chick, Court, Western and Northern Africa Database–Sierra Leone 1990-2002, *Air Combat Information Group Journal*, (5 August 2004), http://www.acig.org/artman/publish/article_462.shtml (accessed 19 June 2007).
56. Ibid.
57. Fowler, *Operation Barras: The SAS Rescue Mission: Sierra Leone 2000*, 142.
58. Ibid., 141.
59. Ibid., 141.
60. Ibid., 149.
61. Prins, "Strategic Raiding."
62. Dorman, "The British Experience of Low Intensity Conflict in Sierra Leone."
63. Prins, "Strategic Raiding."
64. Richards, "Sierra Leone–'Pregnant with Lessons?'" 9-21.
65. United Nations Security Council Resolution 1343 (2001), 7 March 2001, United Nations Security Council, http://www.un.org/Docs/scres/2001/sc2001.htm (accessed 18 August 2007).
66. Dorman, "The British Experience of Low Intensity Conflict in Sierra Leone."
67. Douglas Farah, *Blood From Stones: The Secret Financial Network of Terror*, (New York: Broadway Books, 2004).
68. Keen, *Conflict and Collusion in Sierra Leone*, 287.
69. Gberie, *A Dirty War in West Africa: The RUF And the Destruction of Sierra Leone*, 208-214
70. Sierra Leone Web, "Inaugural Address on the Occasion of the State Opening of the First Session of the First Parliament of the Third Republic of Sierra Leone," (12 July 2002), http://www.sierra-leone.org/GOSL/kabbah-071202.html (accessed on 15 August 2007).
71. Keen, *Conflict and Collusion in Sierra Leone*, 288.
72. See the Special Court for Sierra Leone website, http://www.sc-sl.org.

Chapter 5

Conclusion

For the eleven years between 1991 and 2002 terrible civil wars raged throughout Sierra Leone. The destruction caused by fighting left the country without passable roads, destroyed its electric grid, and ruined its school system and medical systems. The wars killed tens of thousands of civilians and maimed tens of thousands more, leaving the great majority of Sierra Leoneans destitute. In this eleven year period, national, regional, and international leaders tried a number of military means to end the fighting and to create lasting peace. Some of the military operations failed on military terms while others achieved greater or lesser degrees of their objectives. The jury is still out on whether the UN and UK interventions between 2000 and 2002 have brought lasting peace. Nevertheless, the military professional can gain a number of insights from the series of interventions in Sierra Leone reviewed in this study that are relevant not only to Sierra Leone, but to potential future military operations in Africa.

Acting Early and Decisively

As General Sir David Richard states in his article, *Sierra Leone—'Pregnant with Lessons'* "…in essence the international community is guilty of too much talk and not enough coherent and timely pre-emptive action."[1] While this is certainly true, it is unlikely that international or even regional political leaders will act quickly with such a sensitive issue as intervening in the internal affairs of a sovereign state. This decision is also the domain of civilian political leaders, not uniformed soldiers. Military leaders will in all probability not be called upon to take action until the humanitarian or military situation has reached crisis proportions.

When the decision to intervene with military force is made, however, two of General Richard's subsidiary points become critical—first, military action must be launched with a coherent plan that includes all the military, national, regional and international actors. Second, and equally important, the intervention must be launched with energetic action, not with the slowly evolving, haphazard, bureaucratic tendencies so evident during 1999 and 2000 in Sierra Leone. Inter-governmental organizations (IGOs) and non-governmental organizations (NGOs) are notoriously unwilling to operate under the control of any military force. At the same time, military forces bring with them an organizational, mission focused ethos that is especially needed during planning and in the early stages of an intervention. Great effort must be expended by both sides to develop a coherent approach to combining military and non-military actions towards the common objective.

Understanding the Mission and the "Enemy"

It is crucial that any military intervention into a situation like that of Sierra Leone be guided by a clear understanding of the situation on the ground, of the political objectives for the intervention, and of how military forces are to be used to achieve those objectives. The provision of humanitarian relief, the observing of compliance with treaty obligations, peacekeeping, peace enforcement or the deliberate attacking of a hostile force each require different types of forces and different types of operations. Shaky cease-fire agreements made between armed factions under international pressure that are not based on the balance of political power and military power on the ground are especially problematic for the intervening force.

The UN's first intervention in Sierra Leone's civil wars, the UNOMSIL mission in the summer of 1998, ended in failure. In fairness to UNOMSIL, their mission was probably impossible under any circumstances. While current conflict management theory usually holds that the conflict resolution process requires the participation and cooperation of all opponents, the ugly reality of rival conflict often undermines the logic of theory. After ECOMOG troops restored the Kabbah government to power the UN hoped that its UNOMSIL observer force could encourage reconciliation between the government and its AFRC/RUF enemies and the disarmament of private militias. It was clear that the Kabbah government controlled only small parts of Sierra Leone and had neither the political ability nor military power to exercise as a functioning government. Despite some statements and willingness to attend meetings, it also soon became clear that the RUF was never going to acquiesce to being disarmed and that it continued to reject the Kabbah government's claim to legitimacy. Given these inalterably opposed realities, UNOMSIL observers had no peace to observe, no willing partners to disarm, and no means to bring the warring factions together.

When the Lome Agreement was reached in July 1999, the UN again intervened. The UN had learned some lessons from the year before. This time the UNAMSIL mission was chartered under Chapter VII of the UN Charter, was formed around what appeared to be a fairly robust military force, and was given the mission to directly assist the disarmament and reconstruction functions specified in the Lome Agreement. Once again, however, the Lome agreement was based on the false assumptions that the RUF was prepared to disarm and share power in a democratic government, and that the Kabbah government was interested in welcoming the RUF and its political arm into civil society. The Lome Agreement was also very unpopular on the streets of Freetown because RUF leaders were not held accountable for the atrocities they had committed. Secondly, the UNAMSIL forces deployed too slowly in Sierra Leone, were poorly equipped, poorly led, and the UNAMSIL commander failed to employ the authority he had been given to use military force when necessary to enforce the agreement. The DDR process quickly broke down, UNAMSIL forces were harassed and taken prisoner, and by May 2000 the situation was desperate.

The conditions for reconciliation between the government and the RUF simply did not exist in the first half of 2000. Power sharing simply was not possible, the military balance of power was still roughly equal, and UNAMSIL was not prepared to change those dynamics. It was hamstrung by the UN mandate to operate as an ostensibly neutral force between rival parties and the reality that most of its forces were Nigerian units which under ECOMOG had actively favored the Kabbah government against the RUF. Finally, there is almost universal recognition that the RUF should have been destroyed, not offered a chance to gain political power at the bargaining table. The RUF, with its nihilistic violence and deliberate acts of atrocities against civilians was simply beyond the pale.

Overwhelming Military Force

The record of DDR efforts in Sierra Leone, whether internally or externally led, makes it clear that reasonably widespread security, imposed or maintained by a superior military force, is a prerequisite for success. Regardless of political agreements and apparent shifts in the military balance on the ground, the intervening power must have the capability and the willingness to employ overwhelming military force. Whether it intervenes to actively support one side against the other, or whether the force acts as a neutral party, it must possess military power superior to any actual or potential opponents. This is not a question of numbers; it is a matter of military effectiveness and combat power. Executive Outcomes mercenaries were few in number in 1995 and 1996, but they enjoyed a tremendous advantage in combat power, tactical skill, and professionalism over the RUF forces. Both ECOMOG and UNAMSIL who later intervened in Sierra Leone in relatively large numbers and were better equipped than their opponents, had their effectiveness limited by internal weaknesses. UN-

AMSIL further undercut its own military power by its self-imposed limits on the use of force. UNAMSIL only became effective in late 2000 after British assistance and after its new commander proved willing to use his force's military power to force RUF holdouts into the DDR process. The military effectiveness of the intervention force must be clearly superior to all factions if there is any hope that they will comply with either the terms of any peace agreements or with the mandates of the intervening power.

The Advantages and Disadvantages of Coalitions

Many leaders have encouraged the use of regional economic, political and military coalitions as the solution to humanitarian crises in Africa. The mantra has been summarized as, "an African solution to African problems." Regional and international forces are sometimes able to assume the "moral high ground" and to use that status to accomplish humanitarian or other objectives not open to individual nations. The Economic Community of West African States or ECOWAS and its military arm, ECOMOG, have shown the potential for fulfilling this ideal. The US and European nations have expended significant efforts to improve the military effectiveness of African nations in attempts to bring this concept to reality. The national military forces from which ECOMOG task forces are drawn, however, will need years of additional training before they are ready to operate on their own.

As Napoleon once quipped, "Give me coalitions to fight," for he was masterful at exploiting their internal political and military weaknesses. Foday Sankoh and other RUF leaders proved adept at exploiting the gaps in the unity of command and effort among Sierra Leonean, ECOMOG and UN forces. Even the mercenary force from Executive Outcomes appears to have suffered from a conflict of interest involving financial ties to the illegal diamond trade that financed the RUF forces it was fighting. Throughout the period covered in this study, the necessity for unity of command and unity of effort could not be clearer. Both ECOMOG and UNAMSIL suffered from a lack of these key elements at different times during their operations in Sierra Leone. The wording of UN resolutions is an extremely delicate art, and the command and control of military forces operating under UN mandates is extremely important if the intervening force is to be effective on the ground. British forces in Operation PALLISER and UNAMSIL forces, once stiffened by British resolve and a revised UN mandate on the use of force under a new commander, demonstrated what could be achieved with a well led military force.

The Danger of Leaving Too Soon

The military forces which intervened in Sierra Leone showed a consistent tendency to cease active operations or leave the country too quickly after appearing to achieve their immediate military objectives. In late 1995 Executive Outcomes mercenaries had driven RUF units nearly out of Sierra Leone but were unable to destroy the leadership. Between 1997 and 2000, ECOMOG forces repeatedly intervened to restore the Kabbah government to power after it was deposed by AFRC and RUF troops. Each time ECOMOG was initially successful but then went on the defensive before decisively defeating its opponents. ECOMOG was also unable to provide government forces with sufficient internal capacity to secure the country, leading to further anarchy. Even British forces who intervened in mid-2000 and who righted the failing UNAMSIL mission, soon found themselves having to rescue some of their own troops who had been taken hostage in the flush of an easy but incomplete victory. In the fall of 2000, the UK found it necessary to conduct a significant show of force and redeploy some of its forces to Sierra Leone to secure the capitulation of the RUF.

National Military Forces

As many nations have learned in the past and are still learning today, only local security forces can ultimately restore and maintain security to a strife torn nation. While a capable and well led outside military force can intervene to establish order, they must soon be supplemented with and then replaced by local units. While each of the outside powers examined in this study made some attempts to train and equip Sierra Leoneans to serve in government security forces, the efforts were haphazard and ineffective. Training and equipping local units is only a short term portion of a very long term requirement that includes the creation of the institutions of modern military forces—schools, training centers, command posts, regulations, logistics and many others. This is an expensive and long term process that temporary coalitions are loathe to accept. Yet without investing in providing the government of a fragile nation with these capabilities, the likelihood for future interventions will remain high.

Infrastructure

Discovering and using key terrain to support military operations is a principle as old as military history. Tied to key terrain is the importance of controlling the limited civil infrastructure in underdeveloped nations of the world. Sierra Leone provides bountiful evidence of the continuing importance of these principles. The Lungi airport, northeast of Freetown and around the large estuary that separates the Freetown peninsula from the rest of the country stands out as being particularly important. It served as the base of operations, which had to be seized by force in some cases, for every power that intervened in Sierra Leone. The so called "horse-shoe" of roads and bridges between Lungi Airport and the capital city of Freetown were also critical throughout this period. Smaller paved and unpaved airstrips across Sierra Leone were also important given the poor road network. The old British airfield at Hastings, between Freetown and Waterloo, proved important in several operations as a helicopter base. In the case of Operation PALLISER, the British also made excellent use of an intermediate staging base in Senegal to organize their assault on Lungi Airport.

The limited road network in Sierra Leone and the towns that tend to lie at the intersection of those roads were of great importance to any force hoping to control the country. The town of Waterloo which sits astride the main road from Lungi Airport to the Freetown peninsula needed to be controlled by any force seeking to control the country. Conversely, if the intervening force possessed helicopters or naval vessels, they could be used to great effect to provide a decisive mobility advantage of lesser equipped forces. Off shore bases of operation also afford the intervening force a secure place from which to command and supply operations, particularly in the earliest phases of the operation. Control of rivers is important since they form much, but not all of, Sierra Leone's borders. They are also important as means of transportation in the interior of the country. The extensive river deltas in the south and southwest of the country are the source of Sierra Leone's alluvial diamonds that are so vital to its economy. They must be controlled and kept out of the hands of rebels and non-state actors.

Role of Neighboring Countries

If, as is often the case, non-state actors are the primary source of instability that necessitated intervention, they must be deprived of the ability to retreat to a sanctuary or to draw supplies and other resources from a sanctuary outside the nation into which the intervention is launched.[2] When the intervening power or powers does include participation from the affected state's geographic neighbors, it is critical that those neighbors be required to deny sanctuary to any fleeing factions. The RUF was born in Liberia with the active assistance of its fanatic leader, Charles Taylor. Throughout the 1990s Liberia provided both support to the RUF and sanctuary whenever it suffered temporary military setbacks. Neighboring Guinea did not provide active support to the RUF, but neither was it able to deny its territory to RUF fighters amidst the swarms of refugees that fled there from Sierra Leone. Not until after 2002, when Liberia itself began to stabilize, did the RUF lose it ability to hide and reorganize there.

Securing the borders of the affected state and supporting neighboring countries to deny sanctuary to fleeing hostile forces must be part of the objective of an intervention. It is naïve to expect armed bands to respect international borders in many regions of the world, and a peace agreement may do little to change their behavior with regard to borders. Whether they are motivated by political objectives, terrorism, drug profits or simple economic exploitation, the intervening power(s) will have to take measures to deal with this reality. In extreme cases, such as Liberia's aid to the RUF, military force may be needed against another state. Of course, this adds incredible complexity to the political process of building political consensus and a military coalition to intervene.

Cultural Awareness and Dealing with Children Soldiers

Sierra Leone was and remains very much a tribal society. The Temne and Mende tribes are the two largest and have alternated in holding power, but there are more than a dozen other tribes around the country that must be taken into account. Irregular military forces such as the *kamajors* formed an important piece of the security puzzle in Sierra Leone, and these units were organized along tribal lines. Sierra Leone's politics, economics and security situation simply cannot be understood apart from a solid grasp of its tribal cultural heritage.

An unfortunate condition in Sierra Leone, and elsewhere in this period, was the widespread use of children as soldiers. Seized at a young age and brainwashed with a variety of fanatical beliefs, they proved to be extremely deadly. All sides used children in this way, but the RUF was particularly brutal in this regard. Many of the atrocities committed in Sierra Leone were committed by child warriors, sometimes drunk, sometimes high on drugs, and sometimes simply fanatical in their actions. Any military force intervening in Sierra Leone quickly found itself engaged in fighting and killing child soldiers. As much as this assaulted civilized standards of behavior, any military force that underestimated the threat from children fighters suffered because of their laxity. The British soldiers from the Royal Irish Regiment who had to be rescued in Operation BARRAS were taken prisoner by a rag tag mix of irregular fighters and child soldiers. Appropriate rules of engagement must be in place at the start of any intervention where this horrific practice is being used.

Final Thoughts

The history of Sierra Leone during the period of this study is one of unrelenting suffering and destruction punctuated by a series of military interventions which sought to restore order and provide humanitarian relief. Sierra Leone was buffeted by all of the forces that lead to the phenomenon known as a failed state, in which civil government simply disappears or is so ineffective that it cannot perform the most rudimentary functions of a nation state. In such circumstances, political leaders have and will no doubt continue to employ military force in attempts to alleviate the human suffering. The study of the military interventions in Sierra Leone provides ample insights, both from failures and from successes. The record of military interventions in Sierra Leone is littered with failures. This study also demonstrates however, that with proper awareness of the situation and an appropriate mandate, with effective military capabilities, and with sufficient resolve, a military intervention can be successful in providing security and humanitarian relief.

Notes

1. General Sir David Richards, "Sierra Leone–'Pregnant with Lessons?'" in *Royal United Services Institute Whitehall Paper 63–Global Challenges and Africa: Bridging Divides, Dealing with Perceptions, Rebuilding Societies* (August 2004), 9.
2. For a discussion of the role of sanctuaries, see Thomas A. Bruscino, Jr., *Occasional Paper 17–Out of Bounds: Transnational Sanctuary in Irregular Warfare*, (Fort Leavenworth, KS: Combat Studies Institute Press, 2006).

Glossary

AFRC	Armed Forces Revolutionary Council/Armed Forces Ruling Congress
APC/APP	All Peoples' Party, also known as APC, All Peoples' Congress
CDF	Civil Defense Force, Sierra Leone local militia forces
DDR	Disarmament, Demobilization and Rehabilitation. A program established under both the Abidjan and Lome agreements. These were intake centers to disarm and re-train former soldiers
ECOMOG	ECOWAS Military Observer Group
ECOWAS	Economic Community of West African States
EO	Executive Outcomes, a South African private military company
IMF	International Monetary Fund
ISU	Internal Security Unit, Siaka Steven's private security force
JFHQ	Joint Force Headquarters
Kamajor	Local leaders, head of CDF and militia units throughout Sierra Leone
LEOBATT	Sierra Leone Battalion sent to Nigeria
NEO	Noncombatant Evacuation Operation
NIC	National Interim Council, established in 1968 as a second counter-coup replacing the NRC.
NPRC	National Provisional Ruling Council
NFPL	National Patriotic Front of Liberia
NRC	National Reformation Council, established in 1967 as a counter-coup attempt prior to Stevens taking office.
NGO	Non-governmental organization
OAU	Organization of African Unity
PARA	Parachute Regiment, elite British infantry unit
RFA	Royal Fleet Auxiliary, British Navy ship

RSLMF	Republic of Sierra Leone Military Forces
RUF	Revolutionary United Front
RUFP	Revolutionary United Front Party
SAS	Special Air Service, elite British Army Special Forces
SBS	Special Boat Service, elite Royal Marine Special Forces
SLA	Sierra Leone Army
SLP	Sierra Leone Police
SLPP	Sierra Leone Peoples' Party
SOBEL	*sobels* or 'soldiers by day, rebels by night
ULIMO	United Liberian Movement for Democracy, rebel group fighting to overthrow Liberian ruler, Charles Taylor. ULIMO operated from within Sierra Leone
UNAMSIL	United Nations Assistance Mission in Sierra Leone
UNOMSIL	United Nations Observer Mission in Sierra Leone
UNMO	United Nations Military Observer
AFRICOM	United States Africa Command
WSB	West Side Boys, Sierra Leone militia group

Appendix A
Sierra Leone Chronology

1462 Portuguese navigator maps the geography of Sierra Leone and calls it "Lion Mountain."

1787 British settlers buy land from tribal leaders and use it for 400 freed slaves.

1898 Hut tax imposed on 27 April sparks rebellion. Britain declares a protectorate.

1914 Railroad links Freetown with the interior region mines.

1935 De Beers obtained diamond mining rights for 99 years.

1947 The British introduce proposals linking the Crown Colony and the protectorate.

1961 27 April–UK grants Sierra Leone independence.

Sierra Leone People's Party (SLPP) and All Peoples Congress (APC) parties formed.

1962 Sir Milton Margai, head of the SLPP, elected President in May.

1964 Milton Margai dies, succeeded by his brother, Sir Albert Margai.

1967 APC leader Siaka "Big Man" Stevens wins disputed presidential election in March.

Stevens arrested by Chief of Armed Forces after election and declares martial law.

1968 Armed Forces Chief ousted in March by senior military officers.

April–Army NCOs stage a counter coup and declare Siaka Stevens as President.

1971 April–Sierra Leone declared itself a republic.

1978 Stevens declares Sierra Leone to be a single-party state with a new constitution.

1985 November–Joseph Saidu Momoh succeeds Stevens as APC leader and President.

APC domination of diamond trade begins, massive corruption in government.

1989 Charles Taylor begins a rebellion in Liberia.

Revolutionary United Front (RUF) formed in Liberia.

Corporal Foday Sankoh becomes leader of the RUF.

1991 March–RUF guerrillas invade Sierra Leone.

Liberian fighters and mercenaries loyal to Charles Taylor invade eastern Sierra Leone.

RUF forces take over diamond rich areas in east and southeast Sierra Leone.

1992 Sierra Leone government services collapse.

April–Sergeant Valentine Strasser stages a coup that topples President Momoh.

National Provisional Ruling Council (NPRC) led by Strasser is formed.

1994 NPRC enlists children to fight the RUF.

1995 May–Sierra Leone hires Executive Outcomes (EO).

December–EO defeats RUF rebels.

1996 January–Strasser ousted in a coup by Brigadier Julius Maada Bio.

Bio restores the 1991 Constitution; elections declared.

March–Ahmed Kabbah of the SLPP elected President.

October–Second EO offensive against the RUF.

November–Abidjan (Ivory Coast) Agreement. A general amnesty is granted to the RUF.

1997 Executive Outcomes leaves Sierra Leone.

May–military officers overthrow Kabbah government.

Armed Forces Revolutionary Council (AFRC) led by Major General Koroma.

Kabbah flees to Guinea, sets up government in exile.

US Marines conduct two refugee evacuations.

RUF leaders join the AFRC junta. Foday Sankoh named vice chairman.

23 October–Conkary Communique signed between ECOWAS and AFRC/RUF leaders.

1998 March–Nigerian led ECOMOG forces oust AFRC/RUF junta in Freetown.

Ahmed Kabbah's SLPP government restored to power.

RUF leader Foday Sankoh sentenced to death for treason.

13 July–UN Resolution 1181 establishes UNOMSIL mission to Sierra Leone.

Widespread atrocities throughout Sierra Leone.

1999 January–RUF launches "Operation NO LIVING THING" assault on Freetown.

January–UNOMSIL force flees Freetown with Kabbah government.

February–ECOMOG liberates Freetown and restores Kabbah government to power.

July–Lome Peace Agreement signed between RUF and Kabbah government.

October–UN Resolution 1270 authorizes UNAMSIL peacekeeping force.

2000 January–UNAMSIL begins deployment into Freetown, General Jetley in command.

February–UN Resolution 1289 increases size and mandate of UNAMSIL.

April–ECOMOG forces leave Sierra Leone.

April–RUF members seize UN workers in Makeni, Kailahun and Magburaka.

4 May–UK begins Operation PALLISER to rescue UNAMSIL.

May–RUF leader Sankoh captured in Freetown and turned over to British.

June–General Issa Sesay named new RUF leader.

15 June–RUF defeated, Operation PALLISER ends, UK training mission begins.

25 August–British soldiers seized by the "West Side Boys."

10 September–Operation BARRAS frees captive British soldiers.

September–New UNAMSIL commander installed.

October–UK launches Operation SILKMAN, show of support for UNAMSIL.

10 November–Abidjan Agreement, remaining RUF forces submit

to the DDR process.

2001 March–UN embargo on Liberian arms and diamond trade.

US leads worldwide ban on import of Liberian diamonds.

2002 17 January–UN declares the DDR process complete.

January–UN establishes Special Court to try war crimes.

January–UN establishes Truth and Reconciliation Commission.

May–Ahmed Kabbah, SLPP, wins election as President of Sierra Leone.

2003 March–Foday Sankoh and other AFRC/RUF leaders indicted for war crimes.

March–Charles Taylor, ex-president of Liberia, indicted for war crimes.

30 July–Sankoh dies in UN hospital in Sierra Leone.

2004 July–War crimes trials begin.

2005 Last UN forces withdraw from Sierra Leone.

2006 March–Charles Taylor arrested in Nigeria and turned over to UN in Sierra Leone.

2007 June–Trial of Charles Taylor begins.

August–Disputed elections between the APC and SLPP.

September–Ernest Bai Koroma of the APC declared President of Sierra Leone.

Appendix B
Excerpts Of The Lome Peace Agreement

Having met in Lome, Togo, from the 25 May 1999, to 7 July 1999 under the auspices of the Current Chairman of ECOWAS, President Gnassingbe Eyadema;

Recommitting themselves to the total observance and compliance with the Cease-fire Agreement signed in Lome on 18 May 1999, and appended as Annex 1 until the signing of the present Peace Agreement; Hereby agree as follows:

Part One: Cessation Of Hostilities

Article I: Cease-Fire

The armed conflict between the Government of Sierra Leone and the RUF/SL is hereby ended with immediate effect. Accordingly, the two sides shall ensure that a total and permanent cessation of hostilities is observed forthwith.

Article II: Cease-Fire Monitoring

1. A Cease-fire Monitoring Committee (hereinafter termed the CMC) to be chaired by the United Nations Observer Mission in Sierra Leone (hereinafter termed UNOMSIL) with representatives of the Government of Sierra Leone, RUF/SL, the Civil Defense Forces (hereinafter termed the CDF) and ECOMOG shall be established at provincial and district levels with immediate effect to monitor, verify and report all violations of the cease-fire.

2. A Joint Monitoring Commission (hereinafter termed the JMC) shall be established at the national level to be chaired by UNOMSIL with representatives of the Government of Sierra Leone, RUF/SL, CDF, and ECOMOG. The JMC shall receive, investigate and take appropriate action on reports of violations of the cease-fire from the CMC. The parties agree to the definition of cease-fire violations as contained in Annex 2 which constitutes an integral part of the present Agreement.

3. The parties shall seek the assistance of the International Community in providing funds and other logistics to enable the JMC to carry out its mandate.

Part Two: Governance

The Government of Sierra Leone and the RUF/SL, recognizing the right of the people of Sierra Leone to live in peace, and desirous of finding a transitional mechanism to incorporate the RUF/SL into governance within the spirit and letter of the Constitution, agree to the following formulas for structuring the government for the duration of the period before the next elections, as prescribed by the Constitution, managing scarce public resources for the benefit of the development of the people of Sierra Leone and sharing the responsibility of implementing the peace. Each of these formulas (not in priority order) is contained in a separate Article of this Part of the present Agreement; and may be further detailed in protocols annexed to it.

Article III Transformation of the RUF/SL Into a Political Party

Article IV Enabling Members of the RUF/SL to Hold Public Office

Article V Enabling the RUF/SL to Join a Broad-Based Government of National Unity Through Cabinet Appointment

Article VI Commission for the Consolidation of Peace

Article III: Transformation of the RUF/SL Into a Political Party

1. The Government of Sierra Leone shall accord every facility to the RUF/SL to transform itself into a political party and enter the mainstream of the democratic process. To that end:

2. Immediately upon the signing of the present Agreement, the RUF/SL shall commence to organize itself to function as a political movement, with the rights, privileges and duties accorded to all political parties in Sierra Leone. These include the freedom to publish, unhindered access to the media, freedom of association, freedom of expression, freedom of assembly, and the right to mobilize and associate freely.

3. Within a period of thirty days, following the signing of the present Agreement, the necessary legal steps shall be taken by the Government of Sierra Leone to enable the RUF/SL to register as a political party.

4. The Parties shall approach the International Community with a view to mobilizing resources for the purposes of enabling the RUF/SL to function as a political party.

Article IV: Enabling Members of the RUF/SL to Hold Public Office

1. The Government of Sierra Leone shall take the necessary steps to enable those RUF/SL members nominated by the RUF/SL to hold public office, within the time-frames agreed and contained in the present Agreement for the integration of the various bodies named herein.

2. Accordingly, necessary legal steps shall be taken by the Government of Sierra Leone, within a period of fourteen days following the signing of the present Agreement, to amend relevant laws and regulations that may constitute an impediment or bar to RUF/SL and AFRC personnel holding public office.

3. Within seven days of the removal of any such legal impediments, both parties shall meet to discuss and agree on the appointment of RUF/SL members to positions in parastatal, diplomacy and any other public sector.

Article V: Enabling the RUF/SL to Join a Broad-Based Government of National Unity Through Cabinet Appointments

1. The Government of Sierra Leone shall accord every opportunity to the RUF/SL to join a broad-based government of national unity through cabinet appointments. To that end:

2. The Chairmanship of the Board of the Commission for the Management of Strategic Resources, National Reconstruction and Development (CMRRD) as provided for in Article VII of the present Agreement shall be offered to the leader of the RUF/SL, Corporal Foday Sankoh. For this purpose he shall enjoy the status of Vice President and shall therefore be answerable only to the President of Sierra Leone.

3. The Government of Sierra Leone shall give ministerial positions to the RUF/SL in a moderately expanded cabinet of 18, bearing in mind that the interests of other political parties and civil society organizations should also be taken into account, as follows:

(i) One of the senior cabinet appointments such as finance, foreign affairs and justice;

(ii) Three other cabinet positions.

4. In addition, the Government of Sierra Leone shall, in the same spirit, make available to the RUF/SL the following senior government positions: Four posts of Deputy Minister.

Article VI: Commission For The Consolidation Of Peace

1. A Commission for the Consolidation of Peace (hereinafter termed the CCP), shall be established within two weeks of the signing of the present Agreement to implement a post-conflict program that ensures reconciliation and the welfare of al parties to the conflict, especially the victims of war. The CCP shall have the overall goal and responsibility for supervising and monitoring the implementation of and compliance with the provisions of the present Agreement relative to the promotion of national reconciliation and the consolidation of peace.

2. The CCP shall ensure that all structures for national reconciliation and the consolidation of peace already in existence and those provided for in the present Agreement are operational and given the necessary resources for realizing their respective mandates. These structures shall comprise:

(i) the Commission for the Management of Strategic Resources, National Reconstruction and Development;

(ii) the Joint Monitoring Commission;

(iii) the Provincial and District Cease-fire Monitoring Committees;

(iv) the Committee for the Release of Prisoners of War and Non-Combatants;

(v) the Committee for Humanitarian Assistance;

(vi) the National Commission on Disarmament, Demobilization and Reintegration;

(vii) the National Commission for Resettlement, Rehabilitation and Reconstruction;

(viii) the Human Rights Commission; and

(ix) the Truth and Reconciliation Commission.

3. The CCP shall have the right to inspect any activity or site connected with the implementation of the present Agreement.

4. The CCP shall have full powers to organize its work in any manner it deems appropriate and to appoint any group or sub-committee which it deems necessary in the discharge of its functions.

5. The Commission shall be composed of the following members:

(i) Two representatives of the civil society;

(ii) One representative each named by the Government, the RUF/SL and the Parliament.

Part Three: Other Political Issues

The Part of the present Agreement Consists of the following Articles

Article IX Pardon and Amnesty

Article X Review of the Present Constitution

Article XI Elections

Article XII National Electoral Commission

Article IX: Pardon And Amnesty

1. In order to bring lasting peace to Sierra Leone, the Government of Sierra Leone shall take appropriate legal steps to grant Corporal Foday Sankoh absolute and free pardon.

2. After the signing of the present Agreement, the Government of Sierra Leone shall also grant absolute and free pardon and reprieve to all combatants and collaborators in respect of anything done by them in pursuit of their objectives, up to the time of the signing of the present Agreement.

3. To consolidate the peace and promote the cause of national reconciliation, the Government of Sierra Leone shall ensure that no official or judicial action is taken against any member of the RUF/SL, ex-AFRC, ex-SLA or CDF in respect of anything done by them in pursuit of their objectives as members of those organizations, since March 1991, up to the time of the signing of the present Agreement. In addition, legislative and other measures necessary to guarantee immunity to former combatants, exiles and other persons, currently outside the country for reasons related to the armed conflict shall be adopted ensuring the full exercise of their civil and political rights, with a view to their reintegration within a framework of full legality.

Article X: Review Of The Present Constitution

In order to ensure that the Constitution of Sierra Leone represents the needs and aspirations of the people of Sierra Leone and that no constitutional or any other legal provision prevents the implementation of the present Agreement, the Government of Sierra Leone shall take the necessary steps to establish a Constitutional Review Committee to review the provisions of the present Constitution, and where deemed appropriate, recommend revisions and amendments, in accordance with Part V, Section 108 of the Constitution of 1991.

Part Four: Post-conflict Military And Security Issues

1. The Government of Sierra Leone and the RUF/SL, recognizing that the maintenance of peace and security is of paramount importance for the achievement of lasting peace in Sierra Leone and for the welfare of its people, have agreed to the following formulas for dealing with post-conflict military and security matters. Each of these formulas (not in priority order) is contained in separate Articles of this Part of the present Agreement and may be further detailed in protocols annexed to the Agreement.

Article XIII: Transformation and New Mandate of ECOMOG

Article XIV: New Mandate of UNOMSIL

Article XV: Security Guarantees for Peace Monitors

Article XVI: Encampment, Disarmament, Demobilization and Reintegration

Article XVII: Restructuring and Training of the Sierra Leone Armed Forces

Article XVIII: Withdrawal of Mercenaries

Article XIX: Notification to Joint Monitoring Commission

Article Notification to Military Commands.

Article XIII: Transformation And New Mandate of ECOMOG

1. Immediately upon the signing of the present Agreement, the parties shall request ECOWAS to revise the mandate of ECOMOG in Sierra Leone as follows:

(i) Peacekeeping;

(ii) Security of the State of Sierra Leone; Protection of UNOMSIL; Protection of Disarmament, Demobilization and Reintegration personnel.

2. The Government shall, immediately upon the signing of the present Agreement, request ECOWAS for troop contributions from at least two additional countries. The additional contingents shall be deployed not later than 30 days from the date of signature of the present Agreement. The Security Council shall be requested to provide assistance in support of ECOMOG.

3. The Parties agree to develop a timetable for the phased withdrawal of ECOMOG, including measures for securing all of the territory of Sierra Leone by the restructured armed forces. The phased withdrawal of

ECOMOG will be linked to the phased creation and deployment of the restructured armed forces.

Article XIV: New Mandate of UNOMSIL

The UN Security Council is requested to amend the mandate of UNOMSIL to enable it to undertake the various provisions outlined in the present Agreement.

Article XV: Security Guarantees For Peace Monitors

1. The Government of Sierra Leone and the RUF/SL agree to guarantee the safety, security and freedom of movement of UNOMSIL Military Observers throughout Sierra Leone. This guarantee shall be monitored by the Joint Monitoring Commission.

2. The freedom of movement includes complete and unhindered access for UNOMSIL Military Observers in the conduct of their duties throughout Sierra Leone. Before and during the process of Disarmament, Demobilization and Reintegration, officers and escorts to be provided by both Parties shall be required to facilitate this access.

3. Such freedom of movement and security shall also be accorded to non-military UNOMSIL personnel such as Human Rights Officers in the conduct of their duties. These personnel shall, in most cases, be accompanied by UNOMSIL Military Observers.

Article XVI: Encampment, Disarmament, Demobilization and Reintegration

1. A neutral peace keeping force comprising UNOMSIL and ECOMOG shall disarm all combatants of the RUF/SL, CDF, SLA and paramilitary groups. The encampment, disarmament and demobilization process shall commence within six weeks of the signing of the present Agreement in line with the deployment of the neutral peace keeping force.

2. The present SLA shall be restricted to the barracks and their arms in the armory and their ammunitions in the magazines and placed under constant surveillance by the neutral peacekeeping force during the process of disarmament and demobilization.

3. UNOMSIL shall be present in all disarmament and demobilization locations to monitor the process and provide security guarantees to all ex-combatants.

4. Upon the signing of the present Agreement, the Government of Si-

erra Leone shall immediately request the International Community to assist with the provision of the necessary financial and technical resources needed for the adaptation and extension of the existing Encampment, Disarmament, Demobilization and Reintegration Program in Sierra Leone, including payment of retirement benefits and other emoluments due to former members of the SLA.

Article XVII: Restructuring And Training Of The Sierra Leone Armed Forces

1. The restructuring, composition and training of the new Sierra Leone armed forces will be carried out by the Government with a view to creating truly national armed forces, bearing loyalty solely to the State of Sierra Leone, and able and willing to perform their constitutional role.

2. Those ex-combatants of the RUF/SL, CDF and SLA who wish to be integrated into the new restructured national armed forces may do so provided they meet established criteria.

3. Recruitment into the armed forces shall reflect the geo-political structure of Sierra Leone within the established strength.

Part Six: Implementation Of The Agreement

Article XXXII: Joint Implementation Committee

A Joint Implementation Committee consisting of members of the Commission for the Consolidation of Peace (CCP) and the Committee of Seven on Sierra Leone, as well as the Moral Guarantors, provided for in Article XXXIV of the present Agreement and other international supporters shall be established. Under the chairmanship of ECOWAS, the Joint Implementation Committee shall be responsible for reviewing and assessing the state of implementation of the Agreement, and shall meet at least once every three months. Without prejudice to the functions of the Commission for the Consolidation of Peace as provided for in Article VI, the Joint Implementation Committee shall make recommendations deemed necessary to ensure effective implementation of the present Agreement according to the Schedule of Implementation, which appears as Annex 5.

Article XXXIII: Request For International Involvement

The parties request that the provisions of the present Agreement affecting the United Nations shall enter into force upon the adoption by the UN Security Council of a resolution responding affirmatively to the request made in this Agreement. Likewise, the decision-making bodies of the other international organizations concerned are requested to take similar action, where appropriate.

Article XXXVII: Entry Into Force

The present Agreement shall enter into force immediately upon its signing by the Parties.

Done in Lome this seventh day of the month of July 1999 in twelve (12) original texts in English and French, each text being equally authentic.

Alhaji Ahmad Tejan Kabbah, President of the Republic of Sierra Leone

Corporal Foday Saybana Sankoh, Leader of the Revolutionary United Front of Sierra Leone

His Excellency Gnassingbe Eyadema, President of the Togolese Republic, Chairman of ECOWAS

His Excellency Blaise Compaore, President of Burkina Faso

His Excellency Dahkpanah Dr. Charles Ghankey Taylor, President of the Republic of Liberia

His Excellency Olusegun Obasanjo, President and Commander-in-Chief of the Armed Forces of the Federal Republic of Nigeria

His Excellency Youssoufou Bamba, Secretary of State of Cote d'Ivoire

His Excellency Victor Gbeho, Minister of Foreign Affairs of the Republic of Ghana

Mr. Roger Laloupo, Representative of the ECOWAS Special Representative

Ambassador Francis G. Okelo, Executive Secretary of the United Nations Secretary General

Ms. Adwoa Coleman, Representative Organization of African Unity

Dr. Moses K. Z. Anafu, Representative of the Commonwealth of Nations

Bibliography

Books

Abdullah, Ibrahim, ed. *Between Democracy and Terror*. Oxford: African Books Collection, 2004.

Beah, Ishmael. *A Long Way Gone: Memoirs of a Boy Soldier*. New York: Sarah Crichton Books, 2007.

Bruscino, Thomas A. Jr. *Occasional Paper 17–Out of Bounds: Transnational Sanctuary in Irregular Warfare*. Fort Leavenworth, KS: Combat Studies Institute Press, 2006.

Bundu, Abass. *Democracy by Force?: A study of international military intervention in the conflict in Sierra Leone from 1991-2000*. London: Universal Publishers, 2001.

Campbell, Greg. *Blood Diamonds: Tracing the Deadly Path of the World's Most Precious Stones*. Bolder CO: Westview Press, 2002.

Conteh-Morgan, Earl and Mac Dixon-Fyle. *Sierra Leone at the End of the Twentieth Century*. New York: Peter Lang Publishing, Inc, 1999.

Cox, Thomas S. *Civil Military Relations in Sierra Leone: A Case Study of African Soldiers in Politics*. Cambridge, MA: Harvard University Press, 1976.

Farah, Douglas. *Blood From Stones: The Secret Financial Network of Terror*. New York: Broadway Books, 2004.

Fowler, William. *Operation Barras: The SAS Rescue Mission: Sierra Leone 2000*. London: Orion Publishing, 2004.

Hirsch, John L. *Sierra Leone: Diamonds and the Struggle for Democracy*. Boulder, CO: Lynne Rienner Publishers, 2001.

Gberie, Lansana. *A Dirty War in West Africa: The RUF And the Destruction of Sierra Leone*. Bloomington, IN: Indiana University Press, 2005.

Keen, David. *Conflict and Collusion in Sierra Leone*. New York: Palgrave Publishers, 2005.

Kup, Alexander Peter. *Sierra Leone*. New York: St. Martin's Press, 1975.

Lahneman, William J. *Military Intervention: Cases in Context for the Twenty-First Century*. Oxford: Rowman & Littlefield Publishers, Inc, 2004.

Nuarmah, Kwaku and William Zartman. "Intervention in Sierra Leone," in *Military Intervention: Cases in Context for the Twenty-First Century*, William J. Lahneman. New York: Rowmann and Littlefield, 2004.

Prins, Gwyn. *The Heart of War: On Power, Conflict and Obligation in the Twenty-First Century*. New York: Routledge Publishing, 2002.

Schama, Simon. *Rough Crossings: Britain, the Slaves and the American Revolution.* United Kingdom: Ecco Press, 2006).

Journal Articles

Abraham, Arthur. "Mende Government and Politics Under Colonial Rule: A Historical Study of Political Change in Sierra Leone 1890-1937." *The International Journal of African Historical Studies*, VII, 1, (1974). http://www.jstor.org/sici?sici=0361-7882(1982)15%3A2%3C297%3AMGAPUC%3E2.0.CO%3B2-H (accessed 18 June 2007).

Adebajo, Adekeye. "Building Peace in West Africa: Liberia, Sierra Leone, and Guinea-Bissau." *African Studies Quarterly–Online Journal of African Studies*. http://www.africa.ufl.edu/asq/v7/v7i4a11.htm (accessed 10 August 2007).

Bangura, Yusuf. "Reflections on the Abidjan Peace Accord." *Africa Development*, vol. XXII, Numbers 3 & 4, 1997. Council for the Development of Social Science Research in Africa. http://www.codesria.org/Links/Publications/ad_contents/3&4_1997.htm (accessed 10 July 2007).

Chawla, Shalini. "United Nations Mission in Sierra Leone: A Search for Peace." *Strategic Analysis: A Monthly Journal of the IDSA*, Vol. XXIV No. 9 (December 2000). http://www.ciaonet.org/olj/sa/sa_dec00chs01.html (accessed 10 August 2007).

Cooper, Tom and Court Chick, Court. "Western and Northern Africa Database–Sierra Leone 1990-2002." *Air Combat Information Group Journal*, (5 August 2004). http://www.acig.org/artman/publish/article_462.shtml (accessed 19 June 2007).

Dorman, Andrew. "The British Experience of Low Intensity Conflict in Sierra Leone." *Defense and Security Analysis Journal*, Volume 23, Number 2 (June 2007). http://www.ingentaconnect.com/content/routledg/cdan/2007/00000023/00000002 (accessed 8 August 2007).

Ero, Comfort. "ECOMOG: A model for Africa?" *Institute for Security Studies Monograph Series*, no. 46 (February 2000). http://www.iss.co.za/Pubs/Monographs/No46/Ecomog.html (accessed 10 August 2007).

Galic, Mirna. "Into the Breach: An Analysis of the United Nations Mission in Sierra Leone." *Stanford Journal of International Relations*. http://www.stanford.edu/group/sjir/3.1.04_galic.html (accessed 18 August 2007).

Howe, Herbert M. "Private Security Forces and African Stability: The Case of Executive Outcomes." *The Journal of Modern African Studies*, Vol 36, No. 2, (June 1998). http://www.jstor.org/sici?sici=0022-278X(199806)36%3A2%3C307%3APSFAAS%3E2.0.CO%3B2-4 (accessed 18 May 07).

Maanen, Michael van. "Saving the Sum of Things for Pay: Executive Outcomes in Sierra Leone," *Incite: Journal of Political Opinion and Analysis*. http://www.geocities.com/CollegePark/Square/6130/archive.htm (accessed 11 July 2007).

Malan, Mark, Phenyo Rakate, and Angela McIntyre. "Peacekeeping in Sierra Leone: UNAMSIL Hits the Home Straight– Chapter 7: Disarmament, Demobilization, and Reintegration." *Institute for Security Studies Monograph Series*, no. 68. http://www.iss.co.za/Pubs/Monographs/No68/Chap7.html (accessed 7 August 2007).

Montague, Dena. "The Business of War and the Prospects for Peace in Sierra Leone." *The Brown Journal of World Affairs*, (Spring 2002, Volume IX, Issue 1). http://www.worldpolicy.org/projects/arms/news/brown.pdf (accessed 8 August 2007).

Richards, General Sir David. "Sierra Leone–'Pregnant with Lessons?'" *Royal United Services Institute Whitehall Paper 63–Global Challenges and Africa: Bridging Divides, Dealing with Perceptions, Rebuilding Societies* (August 2004).

_____. "Expeditionary Operations: Sierra Leone–Lessons For the Future." *Royal United Services Institute–World Defence Systems*, Issue Four. http://www.sovereign-publications.com/wds-4-articles.htm (accessed 10 August 2007).

Temple, Donald. "Sierra Leone: An Obscure Battlefield in the War on Terrorism," *The Jamestown Foundation*. http://www.jamestown.org/terrorism/news/article.php?articleid=2369857&orubttgus=1 (accessed 15 June 2007).

Newspaper Articles

Shawcross, William. "Sierra Leone Defies Fear and Heads for the Polls." *International Herald Tribune*, 15 March 1996. http://www.iht.com/articles/1996/03/15/edshaw.t.php (accessed 10 June 2007).

Reports

Annan, Kofi. "Eighth Report of the Secretary-General on the United Nations Observer Mission in Sierra Leone." *Reports Of The Secretary-General To The Security Council In 1999*, para. 36. http://www.un.org/Docs/sc/reports/1999/sgrep99.htm (accessed 18 August 2007).

Amnesty International. "Sierra Leone: 1998–A Year of Atrocities Against Civilians," November 1998. http://web.amnesty.org/library/Index/engAFR510221998 (accessed 3 August 2007).

Human Rights Watch. *The Scars of Death*. http://www.hrw.org/reports/2001/children/9.htm (accessed 18 July 2007).

Nuarmah, Kwaku and William Zartman. "Case Study: Intervention in Sierra Leone." Center for International and Security Studies at Maryland (CISSM). http://www.cissm.umd.edu/papers/files/sera_leone.pdf (accessed 3 August 2007).

Truth and Reconciliation Commission of Sierra Leone. *Final Report of the Truth and Reconciliation Commission of Sierra Leone*, Chapter 3. http://trcsierraleone.org/drwebsite/publish/v3a-c1.shtml (accessed 26 July 2007).

United Nations Department of Peacekeeping Operations. *Sierra Leone–UNOMSIL*. The United Nations. http://www.un.org/Depts/DPKO/Missions/unomsil/UnomsilF.html (accessed 3 August 2007).

United Nations, *Human Development Reports*, http://hdr.undp.org/hdr2006/statistics/countries/country_fact_sheets/cty_fs_SLE.html (accessed 20 June 2007).

United Nations Security Council. *Third report of the Secretary-General on the United Nations mission in Sierra Leone, S/2000/186*, 7 March 2000, paragraph 10. http://www.un.org/Docs/sc/reports/2000/sgrep00.htm (accessed 10 August 2007).

United Nations Security Council. *Fourth Report of the Secretary-General on the United Nations Mission in Sierra Leone, S/2000/455*, 19 May 2000, paragraph 17. http://www.un.org/Docs/sc/reports/2000/sgrep00.htm (accessed 10 August 2007).

US Department of State. Bureau of American Affairs. *Background Note: Sierra Leone*. http://www.state.gov/r/pa/ei/bgn/5475.htm (accessed 13 June 2007).

CD-ROM

Vickery, Kenneth P. *The African Experience From "Lucy" to Mandela* Course No. 8678. The Teaching Company. CD-ROM. 2007.

Dissertations and Unpublished Papers

Leatherwood, David. *The Hazards of Strange Bedfellows: The United States, Nigeria, and Peacekeeping in West Africa*. Washington DC: National War College, 2000. http://www.ndu.edu/library/n2/n01LeatherwoodHazards.doc (accessed 3 August 2007).

Pratt, David, MP. *Sierra Leone: The Forgotten Crisis*. Report to Canadian Minister of Foreign Affairs, Lloyd Axworthy, PC, MP, 23 April 1999.

Prins, Gwyn. "Strategic Raiding." Combat Studies Institute, Fort Leavenworth, KS.

Sesay, M. A. "Interdependence and Dependency in the Political Economy of Sierra Leone." PhD. diss., University of Southampton, 1993.

Internet Resources

Ajambo, Eunice. "Debate Over al Qaeda's Connection to West Africa's Diamond Trade Takes New Turns," *allAfrica.com*, 5 August 2004. http://allafrica.com/stories/printable/200408050800.html (accessed 12 June 2007).

BBC. "UK Captives 'Did Not Liaise with UN'–30 August 2000." BBC News Web site. http://news.bbc.co.uk/2/hi/africa/902266.stm (accessed 10 August 2007).

_____. "Sierra Leone Timeline–31 August 2000." BBC News Web site. http://news.bbc.co.uk/2/hi/africa/741070.stm (accessed 10 August 2007).

_____. "Sierra Leone hostage talks 'going well'–4 September 2000." BBC News Web site. http://news.bbc.co.uk/2/hi/africa/909045.stm (accessed 10 August 2007).

Bowles, William. "Executive Outcomes: Tony Blair's Pet Bulldog? The Curious Case of Tim Spicer," posted 18 August 2004. http://www.williambowles.info/ini/ini-0266.html (accessed on 11 July 2007).

Central Intelligence Agency. "CIA World Factbook–Sierra Leone." https://www.cia.gov/library/publications/the-world-factbook/geos/sl.html (accessed 18 June 2007).

CNN Interactive. "Sierra Leone Fighting Eases, Allowing More Evacuations–3 June 1997." Cable News Network. http://www.cnn.com/WORLD/9706/03/sierra.leone (accessed 8 August 2007).

Conciliation Resources. "Profiles–Sierra Leone." http://www.c-r.org/our-work/accord/sierra-leone/profiles.php (accessed 8 August 2007).

Davis, Victor A. B. *Will Sierra Leone Grow Again?* http://www.gdnet.org/pdf/draft_country_studies/SierraLeone-DaviesFR.pdf (accessed 10 June 2007).

Gott, Richard Gott. "Sierra Leone and New Labor Militarism." *Z Magazine.* http://www.zmag.org/crisiscurevts/sierra_leone.htm (accessed 18 June 2007).

Royal Navy. "Argyll Saves 58 From Drowning." *Navy News–Online.* http://www.navynews.co.uk/articles/2000/0008/0000082501.asp (accessed 15 August 2007).

Sierra Leone Web. "Inaugural Address on the Occasion of the State Opening of the First Session of the First Parliament of the Third Republic of Sierra Leone," (12 July 2002). http://www.sierra-leone.org/GOSL/kabbah-071202.html (accessed on 15 August 2007).

_____. "Sierra Leone News Archive, 29 March 1996." http://www.sierra-leone.org/slnews0396.html (accessed 8 July 2007).

_____. "Testimony of Joseph Melrose, 13 February 02." http://www.sierra-leone.org/melrose021301.html (accessed 15 June 2007).

Smillie, Ian, Lansana Gberie, and Ralph Hazleton. "The Heart of the Matter: Sierra Leone, Diamonds & Human Security." *Insights, Partnership Africa Canada*, January 2000. http://www.sierra-leone.org/heartmatter.html (accessed 8 June 2007).

Treaties and Peace Accords

"The Abidjan Peace Accord," 30 November 1996. *Peace Agreement between the Government of the Republic of Sierra Leone and the Revolutionary United Front of Sierra Leone (RUF/SL)*. http://www.sc-sl.org/abidjanaccord.html (accessed 10 July 2007).

United States Institute of Peace. "Economic Community of West African States six-month peace plan for Sierra Leone (23 October 1997-22 April 1998), 23 October 1997." Peace Agreements Digital Collection: Sierra Leone. http://www.usip.org/library/pa/sl/sl_ecowas_10231997.html (accessed 3 August 2007).

UN Security Council Resolutions

United Nations Security Council Resolution 1270 (1999), 22 October 1999. United Nations Security Council. http://www.un.org/Docs/scres/1999/sc99.htm (accessed 18 August 2007).

United Nations Security Council Resolution 1289 (2000), 7 February 2000. United Nations Security Council. http://www.un.org/Docs/scres/2000/sc2000.htm (accessed 18 August 2007).

United Nations Security Council Resolution 1299 (2000), 19 May 2000. United Nations Security Council. http://www.un.org/Docs/scres/2000/sc2000.htm (accessed 18 August 2007).

United Nations Security Council Resolution 1343 (2001), 7 March 2001. United Nations Security Council. http://www.un.org/Docs/scres/2001/sc2001.htm (accessed 18 August 2007).

About the Authors

Chaplain (Lieutenant Colonel) Larry Woods retired from the US Army in 2006 and joined the Research and Publications team of the Combat Studies Institute in May 2007. Prior to his retirement, he served in the Chaplain Corps Branch with the great Soldiers of the US Army in various assignments around the world, including Operation IRAQI FREEDOM. He received his Bachelor of Arts in Philosophy from Ottawa University, his Master of Divinity in Church History from Central Theological Seminary, and his Master of Business Administration in Military Management from Touro University. He is currently working on his Master of Arts in History from American Military University. He resides with his family in Leavenworth, Kansas.

Colonel Timothy R. Reese is an Armor officer and Army historian. He was commissioned in 1981 from the United States Military Academy and has held a variety of command and staff positions in the United States, Germany, Kosovo, and Afghanistan. Colonel Reese holds a Master of History degree from the University of Michigan and a Master of National Security Studies from the US Army War College. He has been the director of the Combat Studies Institute since 2005 and will deploy to Iraq in 2008.